FOUR MEN SHAKING

FOUR MEN SHAKING

Searching for Sanity with
Samuel Beckett, Norman Mailer,
and My Perfect Zen Teacher

LAWRENCE SHAINBERG

SHAMBHALA · Boulder · 2019

Shambhala Publications, Inc.
4720 Walnut Street
Boulder, Colorado 80301
www.shambhala.com

9 8 7 6 5 4 3 2 1

First Edition
Printed in the United States of America

❦ This edition is printed on acid-free paper that meets the
American National Standards Institute z39.48 Standard.

♻ This book is printed on 30% postconsumer recycled paper.
For more information please visit www.shambhala.com.

Shambhala Publications is distributed worldwide by
Penguin Random House, Inc., and its subsidiaries.

LIBRARY OF CONGRESS CATALOGING-IN-PUBLICATION DATA
NAMES: Shainberg, Lawrence, 1936– author.
TITLE: Four men shaking: searching for sanity with Samuel Beckett,
    Norman Mailer, and my perfect Zen teacher/ Lawrence Shainberg.
DESCRIPTION: First edition. | Boulder: Shambhala, 2019.
IDENTIFIERS: LCCN 2018049034 | ISBN 9781611807295 (pbk.: alk. paper)
SUBJECTS: LCSH: Shainberg, Lawrence, 1936– | Spiritual life—Zen Buddhism.
CLASSIFICATION: LCC BQ986.A42 A3 2019 | DDC 294.3/927092 [B]—dc23
LC record available at https://lccn.loc.gov/2018049034

FOR VIVIAN

THE TEARS stream down my cheeks from my unblinking eyes. What makes me weep so? There is nothing saddening here. Perhaps it is liquefied brain.

—SAMUEL BECKETT, *The Unnamable*

CONTENTS

ONE

Roshi dozes in the front seat. Watching him from the back, my eyes are fixed on his bald head as if concentration alone will ease me out of my confusion. I'm stunned by the shift in my state of mind. Half an hour ago, waiting for him to come out of customs, I enjoyed the equanimity I always felt when about to meet up with him again. After all, he was my teacher. The connection I was about to resume was not just with one irascible Japanese monk but with the faith and confidence I found, almost every time, when I sat on my cushion, straightened my back, followed my breath, and believed—yes, again and again—that I was escaping the tyranny of my brain. What has changed since that moment? Why do I feel I'm collapsing somehow, that any thought I'm about to have will only deepen my confusion? And why does this surprise me? This is Zen, isn't it? How many times have I realized that there are regions in my brain that resist my escape from it? That these regions seem to be exactly the ones I need when—as now—I sit at my desk and try to believe in the sentences I produce? Confusion? Better to call it neurological dysfunction. Unless I've experienced a radical cure for that dysfunction, any moment I'll resume the state of mind I lost a few minutes ago.

The head drops quickly. Roshi is fast asleep before we leave the airport. He's never been good at air travel, and he's suffered more and more from it as he's grown older. Now, at eighty, the thirteen-hour trip from Japan is almost debilitating for him. If the past is any guide, he'll be jet-lagged for the next four or five days, disinclined to answer the phone or make anything more than minimal conversation, avoiding especially his English-speaking students. His already fractured attempts at our language have further deteriorated since he moved back to Japan five years ago to become the abbot of Ryutaku-ji, the monastery where he trained. True, neither the jet lag nor the language gap will bother him. If the past, again, is any guide, this old monk, now ministering what many in the Zen world consider one of our most important monasteries, will be on his cushion in our little zendo in downtown New York by 6:15 tonight in order to ring the bell, at exactly 6:30, that begins the first of our three thirty-minute zazen periods. Tomorrow morning, he'll be up by 6:00, sit alone for an hour or more and then—ecstatic to resume the sort of chores his monks take care of at the monastery—vacuum and mop the zendo and the four flights of stairs between it and the street-level door to the building.

This is a payback visit. Six years ago, when invited (some would say ordered) to become abbot of Ryutaku-ji, he endured two days of uncharacteristic vacillation—the only hint of ambivalence I'd ever seen in him—before concluding he had no choice. Much as he loved his students and the zendo, his TV (pro wrestling, especially), and his daily walks in Chinatown or Greenwich Village, his first devotion was to his teacher and his teacher's teachers and thus to the monastery where he'd lived for thirteen years before agreeing to his teacher's request that he establish a zendo in Israel (a country he'd never heard of before setting off for it) a few weeks after the Six-Day War in 1967.

He remained in Israel for fourteen years before heading to New York and then maintained our small zendo in Soho for fifteen years before circling back to his point of origin in Japan. To ease the pain of our separation—the range of emotion experienced by students for whom a teacher like him becomes an amalgam of every spiritual, paternal, or neurotic ideal our minds produce—he promised to return for a month every August, when Ryutaku-ji closes. Today, as for the last five years, he is keeping his promise. Along with two other students—an Israeli, Amnon, who followed him to New York from Israel, and a Japanese woman, Kazuko, who found her way to the zendo when she came to New York to study painting—I've come out to meet him in Amnon's van. Now we crawl in hot summer traffic on the Long Island Expressway while Roshi sleeps in the front seat, and sitting in the back with Kazuko, I consider as if for the first time the confusion Zen generates in my mind, my brain, or the mix of the two that one confronts so vividly in sitting meditation.

Kazuko is dark-haired and stocky, a humorless woman in her midthirties with cold, dark, suspicious eyes. Her voice and face give no hint of her thoughts or mood. Though we have no great fondness for each other, we've managed to work together, taking the brunt of zendo chores, valuing above all that we can count on each other to be on our cushions when the bell rings, remaining still through the great range of pain, anxiety, exhilaration, and realization zazen produces, thus finding a kind of respect not far from admiration for each other. She knew nothing of Zen in Japan, but within months of discovering the zendo, she became Roshi's favorite companion. Alone among his students in the United States, she shares his language. After she took an English-for-foreigners course, she became his frequent, barely competent translator when, as often, his English fails him. Like most Japanese I've known, she is guarded about her private life, especially her background in Japan. Though we've known each other for more than nine years and practiced together for countless hours, I know nothing about her current life or her life before that, in Japan. Then again, we've never been in the backseat of a van together, stuck in traffic on a hot August day. While Roshi sleeps, she eases into a surprising, confessional state of mind, telling me how and why she came to New York, how she began to paint as a teenager and resolved early on to study in America, and finally how she found her way to Zen. None of this, as far as I can see, has caught Roshi's attention, but when she turns to her family life, describing a difficult childhood, a family so dysfunctional she was forced to leave home at sixteen, the bald head rises and, barely turning in our direction, sends an explosive rush of Japanese in her direction.

Done with his tirade, the head drops again. Kazuko turns to the window.

After a moment, I can't contain my curiosity. "Is he angry at you?"

Kazuko nods. "Yes. Very."

"Why?"

"He say I losing all my energy to memory."

ARRIVING AT THE ZENDO, we help Roshi upstairs with his bags, then go our separate ways. I hurry home because a mountain of chores awaits me. Out of town for two months, I have to unpack bags and boxes, get my office organized, and get back to work on my book, which has taken much too long and seems to be going nowhere. Roshi's statement about memory doesn't help. How if not with memory can I expect to produce a memoir?

My desk is piled with mail, book bags, and packages. Most of the book bags contain books related to mine. I've mostly disciplined my book-buying habit, but I can't resist anything on Beckett, Mailer, Zen, or neuroscience because it may contain the information I need to break through the hopeless dilemmas this book presents to me. These are my subjects; I can't escape them. My last memoir, *Ambivalent Zen*, brought me more questions than answers. My Beckett obsession has paralleled my Zen practice; my friendships with him and Mailer, his polar opposite, have forced me to look at the way allegiance to both has thrived in my brain. Six years on this book has not resolved these contradictions, but where if not toward contradiction does Zen direct the mind? It's this equation that Mailer abhorred and Beckett cherished. How can I be surprised that a memoir about this triangle seems to be paralyzed?

I cleared shelves for books related exclusively to the memoir, but I ran out of room a few months ago. Stacks on the floor are crowding each other, and my new acquisitions will of course make things worse. In addition to the shelves that contain books, some are devoted to videos—Beckett's plays, Mailer's films and interviews, and, for Beckett, the new CD containing all of his work. There's also a book called *Beckett's Library*, which is an obsessive examination of the books found on his shelves after he died—all his underlining and notations plus extensive research on the impulses that led him to buy them and their eventual effects on his work. Though I've never read this book, I've leafed through it often and almost every time found something that makes me remember the writer who shaped and sometimes paralyzed my work and, by a sort of miracle, became my friend some years ago when I sent him a book I'd written and he responded with appreciation.

Mailer died just five years ago, but his pile is almost the equal of Beckett's. Two of his wives and one of his girl-friends have written memoirs, and every year the Mailer society publishes *The Mailer Review*, which contains essays and memoirs about him. Michael Lennon's definitive bi-ography came out two years after his death, and Lennon's

738-page collection of Mailer's letters was published just a few months ago. In the mail today are four new books on Zen, two on Zen and the brain, and two on the neuroscience of meditation. In the shelves, begging to be reread, are two biographies of Beckett and the first three volumes of his collected letters. The fourth, containing several he wrote to me, is in the mail on my desk. I can't look at these piles without thinking of information glut and the nightmare it creates for writers of books like mine or, more glaringly, Mailer's. He'd been a best-selling author for decades, but at one point he told me that when he sat down to work, he felt like he was "making buggy whips."

I MET MAILER WHEN I asked him to give me a blurb on *Ambivalent Zen*. As with Beckett, I knew the odds were long against me. Though I'd encountered him two or three times socially, I was pretty sure he'd not remember me. Even if he did, there was no reason to think the book would interest him. For that matter, given the pile my book would surely join on his desk, it was far from likely that he'd notice it, much less take the time to read it.

What I didn't know about him was that he was compulsively generous with blurbs. Books had to be very bad to be ignored, and if they were written by Provincetown writers or those who lived nearby, as I did, they had to be close to or completely unreadable.

Six days later, he called to invite my wife and me to dinner. I joined ten others at a long table in the dining room of the redbrick bayside house he shared with his wife, Norris, and, whenever they came to visit, one or more of his nine children and ten grandchildren. Two of his daughters, with their husbands, were with us that night, along with a couple of local friends and a BBC journalist who'd arrived that afternoon to do a radio interview. Mailer introduced us as if we were regulars at the table.

He was so comfortable in the roles of husband, father, and host that it was easy to forget what he was for me. Except for Beckett, no other writer had meant as much, but since he and Beckett were so utterly different, no one could represent better the dilemma I brought to my work. Like him, though with much less success, of course, I'd been a journalist and a fiction writer. A question I sometimes asked myself—why I persisted in the latter when I was so much better at the former—was a question some had asked about Mailer. More important was a related question, one they certainly did not ask about him: Why did my work remain so subjective and self-conscious when journalism offered the chance to escape from oneself entirely into the concrete world?

Ambivalent Zen wasn't mentioned during dinner, but as we were finishing dessert he pointed a finger at me. "This guy wrote a pretty good book. It's called *Ambivalent Zen*. You know why I like it? It shows me why I've always hated Zen."

Amid the laughter that followed, I didn't get a chance to question him, but later, when we said good night at the door, I said, "What have you got against Zen?"

"I'll tell you when we talk," he said. "How about dinner next week?"

As expected, I find Roshi on his cushion that evening when I enter the zendo. What I do not expect, since I assume he needs sleep, is that, instead of dismissing us after the third sitting, he decides to give a talk.

"This morning, I return, I visit New York. Amnon-san and Kazuko-san and Larry-san—they pick me up at airport, thank you very much."

Twelve students sit in two parallel rows in front of him. None of us who know him well are surprised that after twelve years in New York, where almost any well-known Buddhist teacher attracts standing-room-only crowds, his congregation remains so small. It isn't just that tact is a skill he's never learned. He does not care how many people show up, and, among those who do, he is very quick to discern and alienate those he believes to be insincere or insufficiently passionate.

"Every day world is changing. But you practice zazen, I hope, I wish, you discover...nothing change! Always phenomenal world change, change, change. Never stop! So-called phenomenal world. But you doing zazen, you discover your truth, and truth never change. Never! Understand?"

The forty-five-minute talk that follows is typical of him, a mix of spontaneity and discontinuity that, even though I've been listening to him for nearly twenty years, is not easy to follow or, for that matter, tolerate. Ecstatic, at times, depressed at others, my state of mind is unstable and distracted, but I endure it. If I try too hard to focus, I lose him altogether. I am alternately fascinated and impatient with the wild exuberant freedom (or madness?) of his associations, angry at him and myself for being there, then angry at myself for my irreverence. Again and again, however, I sit back and let his words wash over me, and my brain seems to disengage. No thought arises. I am hardly aware of being there. Then I feel exhilarated, powerful, confident until, angry and a little frightened, I withdraw from him again.

Even though these talks (thanks to one of our sangha members, who worked out the technology) are recorded and passed along to us by email, thus available whenever we like to revisit them on our various electronic devices, he does not like them circulated at all. He wants them *here* and *now* and nothing else. These days, I disobey him often, listen to him at my desk or in the car or on a treadmill at the gym. Sometimes it's possible, listening like this, to feel him *here* and *now* again. I always feel a little like I'm betraying him, maybe betraying Zen itself, to subject him to the demons of technology and electronics, but his voice alone can free me of this concern, remind me that I am more than my state of mind, and that Zen is a whole lot more than my ideas about it.

"I hope everyone appreciate this life! I was born human being, thank you very much. My parents, thank you very much. Must appreciate parents. Without them, you never born human being! Must gratitude your life! You sincere, whole world helping your life. But first must believe yourself. If you can't believe yourself, you can't believe Buddha. Can't believe God. Pain come, thank you very much! Maybe you think I'm talking joke. No, I only talk my own experience. I expect pain because pain become good zazen... You think pain not good. I think pain is good for me. I have friend paralyze, how you call it, stroke, cannot walk straight, half his body dead, cannot walk straight. But you—you still have both legs! You happy! Healthy! If you become everything is good, you enjoy your life. Endless! Permanent! Even under cemetery, some worm bite your bone, you have great, endless, your life become happy. Please don't waste your wonderful life... Understand? OK? Good night!"

I⊤ WAS JUST a few months after I discovered zazen, in the fall of 1973, that I took my first step toward institutional Zen. "Nonmembers night" at the New York Zendo on the Upper East Side of Manhattan. The building I entered was a testimony to the work of D. T. Suzuki, who, with his books, classes, lectures, and conferences, had done more than anyone else to introduce Zen to the Western world. This building, meant to nourish the curiosity he'd awakened, had also taken his teachings a great leap further than he had himself—introducing the structured "sitting" practice called zazen, which aimed to concretize the teachings he wrote about. Despite the fact that he himself had trained in a monastery and throughout his life maintained a daily zazen practice, Suzuki rarely mentioned meditation in his books because, as he'd more than once confessed, he wasn't sure that Westerners were ready for it.

The zendo was full that night, forty people sitting on black cushions in two facing rows in a narrow, ascetic, elegant room. I'm sure I wasn't the only first-time visitor who found it intimidating. A large, gilded Buddha stood amid a spectacle of icons, pottery, photographs, and flowers on an elevated altar at one end, and a bowl-shaped gong half as tall as the Buddha sat on a thick embroidered cushion at the other. Monks in black robes directed me to my cushion. With the clap of wooden sticks called *hyoshiji* and the deep reverberations of the bell, I entered a meditation completely unlike what I'd practiced at home. The silence was palpable and aggressive. Right and left, knees on either side were just inches from my own. Until now, sitting on my own clock and inclination, it had never occurred to me that zazen was not entirely solitary practice. In fact, its basic principle is communal. One isn't meant to be entirely alone in it or left to one's own will and discipline. Supporting this view, the energy in the room was energizing and inspiring. It was also intimidating and distracting. No surprise that my body was tense and uncomfortable, both knees hurting from the moment I sat down. The forty-minute sitting was the longest I'd known, my first taste of extreme Zen pain and, because I endured it, my first experience of what is certainly one of zazen's principal teachings—that the pain threshold can be transcended with concentration.

On nonmembers night, by tradition, a sangha member was invited to give a talk. To my surprise, the speaker that night was a writer for whom I had great admiration—Peter Matthiessen. It seemed a kind of magical karma—so pertinent as I struggled to join my practice to my work as a writer—that he of all people was speaking here that night. A naturalist and a political activist, he was one of the few prominent writers who was known to be a serious practitioner of Zen. Like Mailer, he was recognized for his journalism as much as his fiction. He'd done important work on the predicament of Native Americans in the United States, and his novels, *At Play in the Fields of the Lord* and *Far Tortuga*, were widely respected.

Tall and wiry, he was a handsome man with commanding posture and self-confidence, but he seemed deferential, almost shy as he stood before us. He placed his hands together and offered a standing bow. Speaking in a gravelly voice with a slightly patrician accent, he told us a story so dramatic and exciting that it was hard at first to believe in its reality. Certainly, it was a long way from the quiet and safety of the elegant, insular room in which we sat. He'd just returned from a seven-week, 250-mile expedition in the Himalayas, a trek from Nepal to Tibet through life-threatening extremes of landscape and weather, a quest (initiated by the zoologist, George Schaller) for the elusive Tibetan snow leopard. A little over a year later, the report he offered us would become a celebrated work of nonfiction called *The Snow Leopard*. Since his Zen practice was a constant resource in the mountains—his observations of his own mind no less rigorous than his observations of the landscape and phenomena he encountered—the book

would become one of the best of all contemporary, au-
tobiographical accounts of Zen experience, one to which
I would often turn for inspiration and example.

Like *The Snow Leopard* itself, his talk was a riveting
description of his trek as well as the part Zen played in it. It
included an intimate, moving tribute to his late wife, Deb-
orah, who had died shortly before he left for Nepal. It was
she, he said, who'd led him to the practice and introduced
him to the first teacher he encountered, Soen Nakagawa
Roshi. Soen's name was familiar to all of us who sat there
that night. He was a seminal, legendary figure in American Zen. It was he, said Matthiessen, who'd given him (as
he'd given so many other students, including my teacher,
Kyudo Roshi, who was one of his recognized disciples) his
first taste of the energy he'd found in Zen practice and was
able to access in the Himalayas, and it was Soen, more than
anyone else, who continued to inspire him now.

Matthiessen concluded his talk with an expression of
gratitude for his current teacher, the founder of this zendo,
Eido Shimano Roshi. Eido was another of Soen's disciples.
He sat on a cushion at the front of the row opposite mine,
just next to the altar. Standing now, he bowed to Matthiessen. Matthiessen bowed in return and turned toward his
own cushion but then hesitated and turned back to us. He
had something more to share with us, a memory of a crucial

moment for him that, in years to come, I'd remember as a perfect summary of Zen.

"I have to tell you that when I saw Eido Roshi the day before I left for Kathmandu, he offered me a piece of advice that returned to me constantly on this trip and got me through the worst of it. 'Expect nothing,' he said."

After the gong was struck three times, Eido Roshi offered a deep bow to us and took his seat before the altar. Tonight, he said, he would speak to us about the four basic vows that are the foundation of Zen, the commitment that, "whether we know it or not, we honor every time we sit on our cushions."

He rolled the *r* at the end of "honor" and added a syllable—"uh"—to "time." The first Zen master I had encountered, he did not disappoint my expectations—most of them formed, I suspect, by samurai films. Though his body was hidden by his robes, he looked to be muscular and athletic. His confidence, timing, and deep, projecting baritone voice made the mistakes and superfluous consonants of his surprisingly good English seem skillful and dramatic. One day I would get to know him well when I did an article for the *New York Times Magazine* on the monastery—Dai Bosatsu Zendo ("Great Bodhisattva Meditation Hall")—that the Zen Studies Society was soon to build on fourteen hundred acres in upstate New York. By that time, he would be as controversial as he was charismatic, proof that Zen groups, like so many other religious or political organizations, are far from free of the sad effects of power abused. Rumor and scandal would compromise his teachings and accomplishments. He'd be accused of sexual abuse by numerous female students. He was also accused of exploiting and disrespecting Soen Roshi—a very serious charge in the context of Zen's hierarchical authority structure. In spite of this, he would continue to offer teachings that, like the one he was about to offer us tonight, remained durable and profound, an endless source of inspiration for students like myself. Indeed, the fact that profound wisdom could coexist with the dishonesty, indiscretion, and hypocrisy attributed to this man may be a great Zen teaching itself.

Fundamental to Zen ritual and liturgy, the four vows he'd chosen to speak of are constantly recited at monasteries and zendos all over the world. "Every time we chant them," he said, "we express the desire and commitment that brings us to zazen." He paused a moment and then, slowly and dramatically, recited the vows in full.

However innumerable all beings are,
I vow to save them all.
However inexhaustible delusions are,
I vow to extinguish them all.
However immeasurable dharma teachings are,

I vow to master them all.
However endless the Buddha's way is,
I vow to follow it.

One day these vows would be so familiar to me that they seem imbedded in my unconscious, but they were new to me that night. Indeed, I was so mesmerized by the roshi and the atmosphere of the zendo that I hardly noticed their content, much less the fact that, like so much in Zen, each was a logical contradiction.

After reciting the vows again, Eido announced that his talk would focus on the first. "'However innumerable all beings are, I vow to save them all.' Understand? Please pay attention, OK? Examine this vow very closely. First, must understand that in Zen we mean this, how you say, literally. Zen is not halfway practice. Every time we sit, this is our purpose. Save all beings! Understand? Save! All beings! Sounds big, no? Very—how you say?—ambitious. Kind of impossible, maybe. But tell me, please. What does it mean, 'save'? Save a sentient being? You think maybe make him happy, free of pain? Take away his suffering? Solve his problems? No, no! Please listen to me! Zen always more than you think! And less! From Zen point of view, 'save' mean only 'accept.' Understand? Accept! You want to save a sentient being? Accept him as he is! Save yourself? Accept yourself as you are!"

His presentation was so dramatic and his explanation so much deeper and more subtle than the ideas of Zen and Buddhism that had gathered in my mind that I listened in a state of whiteout. When I left the zendo, I could barely remember what he'd said. But when I got to my cushion the next morning, I found "acceptance" waiting for me. Pure energy, a quick shock of insight—it enveloped me like a wave. The thrust of my practice was suddenly reversed. It was as if every breath until that moment had been a sort of hyperkinetic grasping for one or another circumstance or state of mind, all of which had as their common theme to get me to a place or a state of mind different from where I was at that moment. Some imagined future state of mind, that is, instead of the present, things as they were at that instant. Self-criticism, self-improvement, self-absorption. Achievement, ambition, desire. These had been my driving impulses. Now I was suddenly free of them all. Granted (by my own mind!) permission to be in the present moment, I was overcome with happiness, an equanimity unique in my life.

I suspect this sort of breakthrough will be familiar to anyone who pursues Zen or, for that matter, any activity that brings you to awareness of the present moment and the forgiveness it offers. Unless you're very different from me, I think you will also experience the disappointment that follows. The present moment is not an idea. There is an unbridgeable gap between its reality and its recollection, its conceptualization. All this was particularly vivid for me just then. My exhilaration dissolved almost as quickly as I acknowledged it and further retreated as I understood and reified it. The void in which I found myself was extremely painful and not a little frightening.

No doubt we all have our own way of dealing with such pain. My own was intellectual—and neurological. I'd long been interested in the brain, was reasonably well read in the literature, and, like anyone who studied it, aware of recent estimates about the number of neurons and synapses it contained. Ten billion of the former and, according to a recent article I'd read, "more synapses than there are stars in the universe." It seemed obvious to me that the discomfort and distraction I was experiencing was produced by random electrical firing of the neurons and synapses in my cortex. While I'd accepted myself, my brain—as I saw it—had been silent. Now it was all pandemonium. Wasn't it obvious that, for all its complex functions, it was ill equipped to process the sort of equanimity I'd found? How else to explain the void in which I found myself now? How to avoid the conclusion that rose in its wake—that the grasping hyperactivity which acceptance had dissolved was a symptom of a pathology that, like most people, I took to be my normal cortical reality?

Later on, I'd learn that Zen teachings are careful to point

out that, like any other discomfort or delusion, a hyperactive brain can be accepted and—thus—transcended. But at the time I was nowhere near such understanding. By the grace of Zen, it seemed to me, I'd realized that my brain and I were not the same. Though suspicious of this thought, I took the suspicion itself as a symptom, the brain's way of protecting itself from the truth that Zen had brought me. When I went to my desk soon after leaving my cushion and found myself in a state of anxiety, I took it for neurochemistry. Every thought that came to me seemed to be cortical and pathological. Thus understood, my thoughts inspired me. None I'd known since discovering zazen had seemed to me so worthy of a novel. To this day, I can't think of any other reason for the line I wrote.

"'Brain damage,' I said. Then I fell to the ground.'"

Riding the upside of manic-depression, I was convinced that I'd begun a new book. The fact that the line made no sense and aimed toward nothing beyond itself convinced me all the more. I believed I was taking on brain damage at its source and did not ask myself where one might find a more brain-dependent book than one that aimed to take on the brain damage of its narrator. It's true that even such mental cul de sacs, permitting no escape from the present moment, can be accepted, but we can't forget that doing so requires a freedom from self-consciousness that my own brain, at that moment, did not allow. I suspect I knew, even then, that the combination of Zen and Beckett was leading me into the ultimate cul de sac of a passion for cul de sac itself but as you'll see, such knowledge did not help me in the least.

TWO

Ten days after our dinner at his house, Mailer and I met again. I meant to question his odd, contradictory comment about *Ambivalent Zen*, but soon after our drinks arrived, he extended his arm across the table and, abandoning his normal voice and accent for the guttural, faux-southern he favored when trying to drum up excitement for himself, said, "OK, mah friend, loser buys dinner. Let's see what you're made of."

This was Michael Shay's Barbecue, his favorite place in Provincetown. A plain, sprawling fish-and-ribs joint, it looked like it didn't belong here. He liked it during these winter months because it was usually empty and quiet, and because he was obsessed with the waitress who'd just brought our drinks, slid into the booth, and given him a lingering kiss on the mouth.

"God, you look good tonight," he said. "Are you getting something I don't know about?"

"You know there's no one but you for me, Norman."

"We're gonna have to have a date one of these days."

"Any time, Norman. I'm always up for it."

He took her hand. "Because of this woman, I've finally understood women. The less you give them, the more they give you."

Short, thin, and earnest, she was in her midthirties, a Provincetown native, pretty on her good nights, tough and grim on others. He'd pursued her just this far and no further for years. He shook his head as she walked away. "Isn't she beautiful? Look at her ass. Even beneath her skirt, you can see how hard it is." But then, a moment later: "I don't know why I think of her so much. I must look like Methuselah to her. In the old days, I'd be pushing like crazy for pay dirt, but now I can't do anything but look."

He sipped his drink and then returned to his thumb-wrestling challenge. In years to come, I'd see that flirtation and seduction was a game for him, not much different from the one he'd proposed to me. Games in general were not idle pursuits for him. He was serious about poker, had a twice-a-week game at his house. For nearly forty years, an hour or more of solitaire had preceded his return to his desk every day. Boxing had been a passion until he got too old for it, arm wrestling as well. His father had been a serious, problematic gambler. He'd inherited the habit but managed it better. His pursuit of sports betting had been serious and costly, big losses finally turning him toward self-betting, a kind of solitaire, a game he pursued with no less passion than when real money was on the line. Focused on pro-football, he studied teams, statistics, and betting lines, placed bets against himself, and kept a careful record of wins and losses throughout the season. Then too, there was argument. He was so persistent about our Zen and, later, our Beckett debates that they served as a primary medium for our friendship. He was famous of course for his arguments with feminists and other writers, like Gore Vidal, with whom he'd had a legendary altercation on the *Dick Cavett Show* in 1971. In published articles, he'd challenged and criticized contemporaries like William Styron, John Updike, and Saul Bellow. He liked to say that his public and often vicious arguments with his wife were "the best exercise I get at my age." His lifelong pursuit of women seemed a game as well. In addition to his six

marriages, he'd had more short affairs than he could count*
and one of greater length that had seriously threatened his
marriage to Norris.

His thumb was vertical, poised like a bud in a vase.
Cupping my hand around his (thumb wrestling was not
after all unknown to me), I found it surprisingly small
but, unsurprisingly for a man more than thirty pounds
overweight, thick and spongy. Eyes fixed on our hands,
elbows firm on the table, we touched thumbs three times
and began. Circling, feinting, aiming for leverage and the
final subjugation and control, we were totally engaged,
completely lost in the game. I felt his knuckles in my palm,
his fingers gripping mine. My thumb stretched toward his
and withdrew, stretched and withdrew again, and his did
the same with mine. The table shook, drinks and silverware
rattling. Strategy of course was everything. One didn't win
this game on strength but on seduction and evasion. Set
traps, fake surrender by leaving your thumb as if at each
other's mercy, attack, slip away, and so on and so on. After
a moment, Norman's aggression went too far. I offered my

---

*He told me once that at a party he'd recently met a woman he had known
long before. Impressed by their conversation and the memories it generated, he said, "What a connection we have. We should have made it."

"Norman," she said, "we did."

thumb, and he went for it, and I slipped away and pinned him.

Surprised that I'd won so easily, I checked his drink to see if he might have had too much too fast. No, I seemed to have beat him even-up. It may well be that nothing I ever did in the years of our friendship would impress him more than this victory, but, as any friend of his would tell you, he was not by any stretch a good loser.

"I thought Buddhists are pacifists," he said. "How come you're so aggressive?"

I GO TO SLEEP EARLY but wake in a panic, realizing at once that Roshi's talk is simmering in my mind. No label—not "anxiety," not "terror," not even "panic"—seems right for my condition until it occurs to me that this absence of label is exactly the point. I have *directly experienced* the emptiness that was as always his principal subject. It is beyond labels, beyond description and understanding, because it is beyond the dualistic mind.

Insights come in a rush. I go to my desk, open my word processor, and write a series of notes on emptiness. Pause, reread what I've written, and delete it with disgust. Put my computer to sleep and go to my cushion. My agitation grows, but the more I breathe into it—accept it—the more it seems like clarity.

Next morning, I phone Roshi to ask for a meeting. Though he's tired and still jet-lagged, he is agreeable, suggesting tea that afternoon. Awaiting our meeting impatiently, I alternate between sitting and working at my desk, struggling in vain to find a way to talk about the emptiness I experienced, and, convinced that I'll work out my contradictions with him, amazed at the good fortune that makes him so accessible to me.

As usual, the kettle is on the stove when I arrive, the table set with cups and saucers and a bowl of the Pepperidge Farm cookies he's favored since coming to New York.

"Hi, Larry-san."

"Hi, Roshi. How are you?"

"Dizzy! Tired. Sleep maybe two hour last night."

He shakes the kettle, removing the top to see if the water is boiling yet. "Larry-san?"

"Yes, Roshi?"

"What happen your posture? Last night, back bent, head down! Look weak! Discourage! Many times I tell you—back bent, thought come. Chin down, mind become dark! What happen to you?"

"I don't know, Roshi...I've been sitting a lot, but—"

"Sit like that, you wasting lot of energy! Back bent, anus open. I tell you many times, much thought come through anus! Spine straight, anus close, I guarantee—no thought come."

"I know, Roshi. I know. But sometimes, I guess, I—"

"When you breathe, you all out or only part?"

"What?"

"How you say, 'exhale'? Must not all. If air all out, thought come! Better you keep a little. No space, no thought! You want tea?"

"Yes, please."

Taking a chair, I feel disoriented. It isn't just that, as usual when I meet with him, I've forgotten what I meant to talk about. It occurs to me as if for the first time that I've chosen a teacher for whom thought's arrival in the brain is considered an unfortunate development. How can I be surprised that, more and more often, when I take my seat on the cushion, I feel I'm leaving my work behind?

Using a bamboo strainer, he spoons tea from a silver can I recognize. This is high-quality *sencha*, grown on a small farm owned by the monastery. When I'd lived there—for a month—two years before, I'd joined the training monks to help in its harvest. Six days on hands and knees, picking it leaf by leaf, like mowing a lawn by hand. Like so much Zen practice, a great test for one's boredom threshold. No other tea cleared my head so quickly or better helped my zazen. One sip now reminds me why I'd called him this morning.

"Roshi?"

"Yes?"

"I've got to talk to you about something important."

"Sure, sure. What?"

"More and more, it seems to me my work contradicts zazen. It's like a power struggle, an impossible contradiction. If I pursue my work, I'm no good as a Zen student, and if I'm serious about Zen, I'm no good as a writer. Once and for all, I've got to decide where I stand. My work takes me away from Zen, and Zen takes me away from my work. I've got to give up one or the other. Stop writing and go to the monastery, or stop sitting and devote myself to writing."

Roshi shook his head. "Stop?"

"Yes, one or the other!"

"Larry-san?"

"Yes?"

"I tell you many times—don't keep anything! Beautiful zazen, don't keep. Terrible zazen, don't keep. Stand up, let go. Good part forget, bad part forget. Both forget! Just this is all! Not so easy, I know. It's easy to practice Zen on a cushion. Five thousand times more easy than off. Stand up, you practice. Eat, you practice. Shit, you practice. Let go, just this, take it! Everything practice! Wonderful zazen, terrible zazen, please don't complain, don't analyze, just take it. If you patience, I guarantee you can do it! No need hesitate. Must believe yourself. If cannot believe yourself, cannot believe Buddha. Cannot believe God. Happy come, thank you very much! Pain come, thank you very much! You and pain, good relationship! Bad writing, thank you very much! Good writing, thank you very much! Maybe you think I'm talking joke. No, I only talk my own experience."

"I know, Roshi. I know. From the point of view of Zen, I get it. But when I sit down to write, I hit the wall. It seems to me that no work in the world is further from Zen than writing. I'm happy when I practice, but how can I go all the way with it if I don't give up writing once and for all?"

"Give up?"

"Yes! Once and for all!"

Roshi pushed the cookies toward me. "More cake?"

"No thanks, Roshi."

"More tea?"

"Yes, please."

"Larry-san, I tell you many times your problem—you attached to emptiness! Formless, empty, good, bad, forget it! Don't keep any mind! If you thinking empty mind, you have partner. Already empty mind become dust mind. If you thinking something, you have picture inside your brain. Then can think! Zazen not only meditation. Your daily movement, meditation; your activity, meditation. Sitting time, just sit. Writing, just write. No need mix up. When you shit, you wipe anus, no? Then flush paper, no? No need keep paper, walk around shit in your pocket. Back straight, no problem! Too much thought, you 'fraid can't sleep, mind dark, sad, become mental sick. I think you have idea of emptiness. Therefore, can attach. Aim for emptiness, like target. But please you understand, Larry-san—target not outside you. You and target, no distinction! No way you can miss!"

THE BRAIN DAMAGE NOVEL would be published as *Memories of Amnesia* in 1988, but it had a long way to go before that. Naturally, my first burst of excitement was short-lived. There were moments of clarity, but they never lasted more than a couple of paragraphs. I was always in pursuit of the experience of acceptance that Eido Roshi had triggered. It was clear to me that it had been a nondualistic experience—which my brain, inherently dualistic, always compromised—but I could find no way around the fact that I needed dualism to write the book. This made it a manic-depressive experience, but I tried my best to take this as its virtue. From a book that aimed at differentiation from the brain, how could I ask for anything better than bipolarity? How be surprised that I was less coherent every day? If I meant the book to acknowledge the discontinuous truth I experienced in meditation, I had to expect discontinuity within my sentences as well as between them.

What saved me from this nightmare was a seminal instruction by the great Zen patriarch Eihei Dogen. "To study Zen is to study the self. To study the self is to forget the self." I'd been familiar with this teaching since my earliest days in the practice, but one night, during sitting, I understood it for the first time. I realized that the various ambitions in which I was trapped—writing about zazen, writing about the brain that produced the writing, writing about the impossibility of what I was trying to do, and so on—were not just self-defeating but self-absorbed. They weren't serving my zazen, and they weren't serving my work. In fact, my work had become the antithesis of zazen, and this contradiction was sabotaging my zazen as well. How could I forget my self when I was obsessed with the brain that generated it? The more I fixated on my neurology, the more it reinforced the self that fixated on it. That was the real brain damage—self-absorption and the fixations it engendered. If I really wanted to understand the brain and brain damage, I needed to break through my self-absorption, let go of myself, look at *others'* brains, *others'* pain and pathology. It wasn't fiction I needed to write. It was journalism. I needed to get out of my office, let go of myself, and meet real victims of actual brain damage face-to-face.

THE SOHO ZENDO was located about a mile south of my apartment and slightly more than two miles north of the World Trade Center. In other words, as I realized on September 11, 2001, its location allowed Roshi to hear

United Airlines flight 11 fly over the zendo on its way to devastating its target in a collision that would change the world.

I had awakened that morning with only one thought in mind—Roshi was scheduled to return to Japan at seven that evening, and we'd not resolved or even discussed an issue that, in my view, was crucial to the zendo. When he left New York and returned to Japan, he had asked me to teach the weekly Wednesday night beginners' class. He'd instructed me carefully in preparation, but while most of what he said was inarguable, there was one thing on which we disagreed. All who came to the class, he said, must sit on cushions on the floor. Though he permitted chairs for veteran students, beginners were not to be offered this option. I wanted to respect his rules, but this one had often put me in a quandary. Among those who came to the class, there were more than a few who, because of age, injury, or other physical limitation, could not fold their bodies into one of the cross-legged or kneeling positions floor sitting required. How could I turn them away? I'd mentioned it more than once to Roshi but found no compromise. "Zen not relaxation, Larry-san. Senior student understand. Zen mind bravery mind! Take your pain! Don't escape! Beginner cannot understand. Big mistake make it easy for them. Must be kind to them. Offer true Zen. Understand from start—zazen not relaxation!"

I understood his logic, but over the past year, I'd allowed five students—one a veteran with arthritis, a new student with runner's knee, two in their seventies, one in his mideighties—whom he would have barred from attending. Turning them away seemed not just irrational and mean-spirited but a contradiction of Zen. Weren't we reminded constantly of the fundamental precept—"Don't say no to anyone who comes, and don't chase after anyone who leaves"? For months before Roshi's arrival this time, I'd promised myself to confront the issue with him. Now he was about to leave, and I'd found no opportunity to do so. On waking that morning, I'd vowed to settle the matter once and for all before he returned to Japan.

Just three miles north of the World Trade Center, my apartment had an unobstructed view of the towers, but despite the fact that they'd long shaped the space and gathered the light of the world I inhabited, I'd taken them for granted. I gave them no thought as I sat that morning or, later, got on my bike and headed for the gym. Heading home two hours later, the call to Roshi uppermost in my mind, I turned onto lower Fifth Avenue and found a crowd in the middle of the street, all eyes fixed on a fire in the South Tower about three miles away. Flames blazed and smoke billowed, but since the plane wasn't visible, the source of the fire was unclear.

By the time I got home a few minutes later, the second plane had struck, and the disaster was visible from my window. Switching on my TV, I heard the first mention of hijacking, the first suggestion that we might be in the midst of a terrorist attack. Standing at the window while I phoned Roshi, I saw the fire spreading, smoke enveloping both towers now, the tails of both planes extending from the upper floors.

"Hello, Roshi."

"Larry-san! What happen? I hear airplane very loud fly over zendo!"

"No one knows, Roshi. They think it's a terrorist attack."

"Yes, I know! I watching TV. Terrible! Terrible! What happen?"

"God knows, Roshi."

"Terrible! Terrible!"

"Yes, it's horrible. No one knows what's going on."

We were silent for a moment, me gazing out my window at the fire downtown, Roshi no doubt fixed on his TV.

"Roshi?"

"Yes?"

"I've been meaning to talk to you about something before you go back to Japan."

"What, Larry-san?"

"I want to allow beginners to sit on chairs."

"Why?"

"I've told you before. Many people can't get down on

the floor. Some are old, some injured. Why should we turn them away? They might become serious students."

"Larry-san! Please! Senior student can chair. Beginner not understand! Sit in chair, think Zen relaxation. Back bent, mind weak. Wasting lot of time! Thinking, thinking, never learn to sit. Zen not relaxation! Zen mind bravery mind. Cheerful mind! Please, Larry-san. Why you not trust me?"

Thirty minutes later, the first building collapsed. Fifteen minutes after that, it was followed by the second. Since airports were closed, Roshi would not depart for three days. Early that evening, realizing that he would be on his cushion at 6:30, I headed for the zendo to sit with him. I found the block permeated by the odors of smoke and death that would fill the air of Lower Manhattan for the next three months. The neighborhood was transformed into a military zone. Barricades and military vehicles blocked my path. Access was barred for anyone who could not produce proof that they lived on these blocks. Returning home, I sat alone throughout the evening, processing the news that the towers, along with the Pentagon, had been attacked by terrorists, the whole of the world transformed by an event so unimaginable that it seemed imagined—a TV show perhaps, maybe a movie. Following my breath through surges of terror and disbelief, I realized, again and again, that terror is not just an external threat. The mind can produce it, all on its own.

I'D DONE ENOUGH TIME in journalism to know how to seek out opportunities and permissions for research, but like any reporter, I found hospitals difficult to penetrate. After several rejections, I wrangled the permission of authorities at a VA hospital to spend time with a patient who was more or less a fixture on the ward. I owed my access to the fact that no one else wanted to be with him. He was dull and incurable, required almost no care, and had not excited researchers or even the students and interns who met him on rounds. They called him "the professor." This was not a pseudonym but a link to his past life. Until viral encephalitis infected his brain three years before, he'd been chairman of the psychology department at a prestigious midwestern university, a respected teacher who'd published widely in his field.

He was a stocky man of medium height who walked the wards and grounds enough to keep himself in fairly good condition. His hair was gray and thin, but he looked younger than his sixty-two years. His dark eyes were fixed—no surprise—in a state of sad disbelief, but his face retained just enough of his past authority and intelligence to make it possible, though certainly not easy, to forget his condition. He was an unusual patient because, even though he'd lost his short-term and most of his long-term memory, he retained his verbal and motor function. He spent most of his time trying in vain to recover biographical information. Despite the fact that his wife and daughter and several former students visited him once or twice a month, he struggled to recall whether he was married, had children, had ever held a job, and, most obsessively, why he could not remember things. Again and again, as if with revelation, he said, "I think I have problems with my memory." This discovery usually led to a long silence and, frequently, to the conclusion that his problem was caused by acid indigestion, which in turn was eased by candy bars. After I understood this and began to bring a stash when I visited, he was always glad to see me, but he never recognized me. If I left his room for even two or three minutes, he'd greet me when I returned as if he'd never seen me before. He liked to cover his deficit with one of two long-out-of-date expressions—"See you later, alligator!" or "After a while, crocodile!"—which, despite his amnesia, he retained from his adolescence.

The hospital was almost two hours away by train. Gray and cheerless, a void of a place, its architecture and atmosphere were not all that different from a prison. As I made the trip that first day, I thought a lot about a writer I'd recently been reading and rereading—Norman Mailer.

I needed guidance and encouragement to make the leap from fiction to journalism—surrendering my subjective obsession with my own brain to an objective inquiry into the brain itself—and Mailer was my perfect muse. He'd made his name as a fiction writer with *The Naked and the Dead*, met critical disappointment with his next two novels, and then written a masterpiece of personal journalism, *Armies of the Night*. That book had required him to leave the privacy and solitude of his office to participate in an event of major historical and political proportions, the October 1967 March on the Pentagon. Though written in the third person, its hero was a perfectly realized character named Norman Mailer, who was ingeniously distinct from the author who'd created him. It seemed to me that Mailer had found his voice by letting go of himself, discovered his vision with total surrender to objective reality. The book he'd produced was a perfect combination of real-world description and novelistic skill. How could I ask for a better example as I set out to explore a world of medical catastrophe, which would surely humiliate my presumptuous attempts to imagine it?

The professor's obsession was solitaire. Arriving with my bag of candy, I almost always found him in the midst of a game. He played hour after hour, all day long, every day, with fixed concentration that was clearly immune to repetition and boredom. Like each candy bar he was offered, each breakfast of each day when he awakened, every game was his first. Since this was before the days of the personal computer, he played with real cards, spreading them carefully on his tray table, which he rolled back and forth between his bed and the orange lounge chair in the corner of his room. As he spread his cards, his vacant eyes came alive with concentration, and the dark sadness of his face gave way to resolve and determination. His disease was a catastrophe he'd never escape, but inside the game, he was free of it.

Devoid of the instrument stands, rolling carts, and beeping alarms that turn most hospitals into auditory nightmares, the neurology ward was silent, almost serene. Three days a week for three weeks, I arrived midmorning with my notebook and a bag of candy and, for two or three hours, sat near the foot of his bed while he played. Thoughts of my book embarrassed me. Both the condition I was looking at and the effects of play on it made my attempt to understand the brain look shallow and insignificant.

Since there was no conversation between us, our routine became a ritual, a period in which I sat in something very like zazen. Nothing settled my mind like watching him play. It seemed to me that, when he placed one card on another, he escaped his brain, arranged his life once and for all, liberated himself from anxiety. Was that what I was doing when I followed my breath, straightened my back, and tried to forget myself? Was zazen after all a kind of solitaire without cards?

After a while there seemed to be no difference between us, no time but the present. I was detached and professional with him, but it seemed to me that our intimacy deepened every day. I can't doubt that it was this feeling of intimacy that led me to cross the line between us.

He did not greet me when I arrived that morning. He was well into his game when I pulled my chair close to his bed. He nodded but did not veer from his cards. He lost that game and the one after that. By the time he was into his third, I had settled into the mind I'd come to expect in his room. I felt as if there were no time but the moment we shared, no difference between his state of mind and my own.

I could see by the speed with which he moved his cards that his third game was going well. *Snap, snap*—the cards came off the deck and found their way quickly to others. As if for the first time, I marveled at the fact that within the game he found an order and peace he could not attain without it. What did this say about the brain? What had I missed with all my obsessive thoughts about it? Were thoughts themselves like cards one tried to arrange?

Within a few moments, all his cards were consolidated in four neat piles near the top edge of his table. As often, the satisfaction on his face was so infectious that I felt it myself.

He paused for a moment to contemplate his success and then quickly collected his cards and arranged them in a deck. Finally, he reached for the bag of candy I'd brought. With no less interest than he'd shown in his cards, he examined its contents and extracted, unwrapped, and bit into a single bar with enthusiasm.

"You won," I said.

"Yes!" he said.

"That's great."

"Yes!" he said.

"How are you today?"

He considered my question for a moment, then shook his head. "Not good. Not good at all."

Abrupt mood shifts were hardly uncommon for him, but I'd never seen his face go dark more quickly. "I'm having problems," he said, "with my memory."

"Really? I'm sorry to hear that."

"Am I married? Do I have children? I'm trying to remember...but I can't!"

Until now, I'd always felt protective of him when he sank like this, trying my best to feel the frustration and desperation he felt. I knew it wouldn't help, but I tried to offer him good thoughts—reminding him of his wife's and daughter's visits, the nurses and doctors who were always available to him, and so on. Just now, however, for reasons I'll never understand, I felt no such urge. It was as if the intimacy we shared made me forget he was a patient and think of him as a friend. In fact, I felt just a little impatient with him.

"Why not forget?" I said.

"What?"

"You spend so much time trying to remember things— why not try to forget them? After all, you've got amnesia. You should be able to do that easily."

"Amnesia?"

"Yes. You forget everything, right? What's the big deal if you can't remember your wife's name? Forget everything and you won't have to worry about it anymore."

He stared at me for five or ten seconds in wide-eyed disbelief. Then he laughed aloud in three bursts separated by five or six seconds. He wasn't smiling. One could not suspect that he found anything funny. Mirthless, hollow, louder and louder, like stage laughter by a bad actor or the "Ho! Ho! Ho!" of a professional Santa Claus, the sounds he produced seemed almost disconnected from him. He'd always been mild, congenial, no threat to anyone, but his face was angry and the laugh aggressive. I left the room quickly, but even at the far end of the long hall between his room and the nurses' station, I heard him bellowing: "Ho! Ho! Ho! Ho! Ho! Ho!" The sound was one I'd never forget, and the fact that I left his room so quickly—literally ran away from him—was an act for which I'd never forgive myself.

THREE

RICHARD DAVIDSON, a professor of psychology and psychiatry at the University of Wisconsin, is one of the pioneer researchers of the neurological effects of meditation. In the first of his books on the subject, *The Emotional Life of Your Brain*, he writes about his initial research in India, which was inspired by the Dalai Lama.

"In the spring of [1992] I screwed up my courage to write a letter to the Dalai Lama. I presumptuously asked the head of Tibetan Buddhism if it would be possible to study some of the expert meditators living in the hills around

Dharamsala, to determine whether and how thousands of hours of meditation might change the brain's structure or function.... [It seemed to me that] the yogis and lamas and monks living in the hills would be perfect for this, because they undertake meditation retreats lasting months or even years, which I suspected would have left a lasting impression on their brains."*

When the Dalai Lama responded positively to his request, Davidson and three colleagues, one of whom spoke fluent Tibetan, made a trip to Dharamsala, where they met with the Dalai Lama and discussed their project in detail. With his recommendation in hand and Sherpas hauling seven backpacks stuffed with sixty pounds each of electronic research gear, they proceeded into the foothills of the Himalayas to meet the closest meditator, a monk who had been living in retreat—in a stone hut ninety minutes from the end of the nearest dirt road—for ten years. Their initial hope was simply to conduct rudimentary experiments, but the monk demurred. "[He] explained all too modestly," writes Davidson, "that his own meditation practice was mediocre at best...and that if we wanted to learn the effects of meditation, we should just meditate ourselves!"

*Richard Davidson and Sharon Begley, *The Emotional Life of Your Brain: How Its Unique Patterns Affect the Way You Think, Feel, and Live—and How You Can Change Them* (New York: Penguin, 2012), 184.

The rest of their inquiries were no more productive.

Over the course of... a three-hour debate, [the next monk told us] it makes no sense to try to measure the mind, which is formless and nonphysical. If we did succeed in measuring anything, he assured us, it would be completely unimportant in terms of understanding the effects of meditation.

This is how it went through monks three, four... through ten. One kindly advised us to pray to the Dalai Lama for success in our work. Another suggested we return in two years, by which time he might have achieved some modest success in attaining *shamatha*, a Sanskrit word best translated as "meditative quiescence," whose goal is to block out distractions so the mind can focus on an object with clarity and stability. Others feared that undergoing our weird tests would disrupt their meditation practice. But the most consistent theme was that expressed by Rinpoche 2: Physical measurements were simply inadequate for discerning the effects of meditation on the mind. Use EEG to detect, say, the compassion that meditation has the power to cultivate? Please. By the time we reached our last monk, we were 0 for 10.*

*Davidson and Begley, *Emotional Life of Your Brain*, 188–89.

Vodka was my first mistake, mention of Zen my second. Vodka because it made me say too much and Zen because once I began I never knew when to stop. I knew that I was headed for trouble, but I was already aware that Norman took over conversations so quickly that the whole evening could slip away on the current of his wit. If I wanted to say something, I had to do it fast. "I've been thinking a lot about thumbs and thumb wrestling. Every time I sit on my cushion, actually."

We were almost alone at Michael Shay's. Our second dinner—he'd called to suggest it. It was gray and cold outside, a typically dismal night in a typical Cape Cod winter. Mailer was wearing fur-lined boots and a black fleece vest, looking older and frailer than the first time we'd met. We were sitting at a table next to the wall, and he'd balanced the two canes he was never without between it and his chair. I explained that in Zen practice you cupped your hands in your lap, touched your thumbs together lightly— "about enough, we say, to hold a piece of paper between them"—and focused your mind on them. "Concentrate intensely and your thumbs bring you to the present moment, things as they are, which in the end is all that Zen is about. Teachers say that all opposites are joined in this meeting of thumbs. All opposites. Both sides of the body, both sides of the mind. My teacher—the one you read about in *Ambiva-*

lent Zen—says that this union is infinite, formless. Heaven and earth, good and bad, light and dark, subject and object, cause and effect. Absolute and relative. Touch your thumbs like this and all distinction falls away. The thrust of your dualistic mind dissolves."

He sipped his drink, eyed me over the edge of his glass, and then sipped again. "I can't believe a writer as good as you would use such language."

Vicki had brought our drinks. Off-season, here in Provincetown, Michael Shay's could not afford a bartender, so she'd made them as well. Mailer was very, very particular about his whiskey sours, but hers, once again, had satisfied him.

"I swear to God, honey, no one makes them like you. You're getting to be a genius at it."

He was affectionate with her as usual but less flirtatious and seductive. In the car, coming over, he'd been uncharacteristically languid, complaining that he was stuck in his work. "I'm sleeping too much, watching too much TV. If I weren't so old, I'd be depressed."

He was eighty years old. Arthritis in both knees made his walk slow and lumbering, the canes an absolute necessity. The extra weight he carried didn't help. His hearing was shot, his eyesight poor, and his breathing was already calling for the coronary bypass he'd need five months from now. None of this, apparently, had affected his work.

He was up at ten almost every day. After a long breakfast (and what his good friend and biographer, Michael Lennon, would one day describe as "a long time on the can") and an hour or more of "combing" his mind, as he put it, with solitaire, he'd struggle up the stairs—with canes of course—to his office on the third floor and work until seven or eight in the evening, every day. "A professional," he liked to say, "is someone who can do a good day's work on a bad day." He'd met this definition for years, and age wasn't stopping him now. "Getting old without cracking," he said, "is the ultimate art form." As always, he wrote longhand and faxed his pages to his secretary in New York City. She typed them and faxed them back the next day. One of the benefits of old age, he claimed, was that he was a better editor of these pages because he could not remember writing them.

He'd written thirty-seven books, a best seller in each of the last six decades, made three movies, won three Pulitzer Prizes, and run for mayor of New York and not finished last. Youth and middle age had been wild, often self-destructive, and much-publicized rides for him. Compromised at times by Seconal and marijuana, his work had known radical extremes of style, ambition, and public reception. As a public figure, he'd been famous for his unapologetic egoism, his public battles with media figures, feminists, other writers, politicians he disagreed with, and, most famously, his second wife, whom he'd barely missed killing when he stabbed her with a pen knife at the end of a nightlong drunk at a party—an event that almost sent him to jail for life. Perhaps it was because of the wild ride he'd left behind that his view of old age was neither negative nor resistant. Of course it had its downside. "I used to boast a roll of silver dollars. Now I'm lucky to have two inches of dimes. This, believe it or not, inspires my pleasure. It's a wan expression of audacity but it's still my own. In the end, aging is not so disagreeable."

He placed his hand on the table between us. "Let's go again."

We moved our drinks aside, curled our fingers into our fists and each other's, touched thumbs again, once, twice, a third time, and then, severe and concentrated, went at it again. He pinned me in less than a minute.

"C'mon," he said. "You can do better than that." But again he took me. Was it embarrassment about my pathetic description of Zen? His put-down in response? Or just the fact that I'd been thinking about the game, about him, remembering it almost every time I sat and brought my thumbs together in my lap? Whatever the reason, I felt self-conscious, disfocused, nowhere near the concentration I needed to compete with his.

We tried again and the result was the same. Focused or not, I was no match for him tonight.

Vicki came over with a platter of shrimp and a bowl of cocktail sauce. His favorite dish. As usual, he'd called to order it for us this afternoon. We'd have shrimp every time we met here until, a few years later, a tooth infection led to a dental nightmare that would require extraction of all his teeth. Since implants were prohibitively expensive, he'd be forced to use false teeth, which he found unbearably humiliating. From then on, we'd have oysters instead of shrimp because, he explained, "I can't dominate shrimp anymore."

He picked up a shrimp and dipped it in cocktail sauce. "The trouble with you," he said, "is you don't know how to win."

SEVERAL WEEKS after 9/11, when I returned to the Cape, I had dinner with him again. A few minutes after we sat down, he offered me his summation of the event. "I'd say this for sure: it was a good day for the devil."

Since this was early in our friendship, I knew nothing yet of his cosmology. As he'd elaborate in the last book of his life, it was very literal about the conflict between God and the devil. What I did know was that a rush of conspiracy theories were already afloat about 9/11, no small number of them focused on the large number of inexplicable co-incidences that had marked that day and, intentionally or not, collaborated with the terrorists. "What do you mean by 'the devil'?" I said.

"What?"

"No one doubts that evil fueled the event, but unless you're explicit in your definition of 'the devil,' we can't know if you mean to be taken seriously."

He shook his head with impatience. "Sometimes I think you don't realize how arrogant I am."

It is in the tranquility of decomposition that I remember the long confused emotion which was my life…to decompose is to live too, I know, I know, don't torment me…

—Beckett, *Molloy*

After my time with the professor, I tried to go back to my novel (*Memories of Amnesia*), but its ambiguities and contradictions were no more manageable than they'd been before. At times, it edged toward comedy, but then the idea of making comedy out of brain damage seemed unforgivable, heretical. Maybe Beckett could play with such catastrophe, but I could not by any stretch imagine doing so.

Another stroke of luck saved me from it again. A friend introduced me to a prominent neurosurgeon named Joe

Ransohoff. He was a colorful, close-to-legendary figure in the world of neurosurgery—practicing, as well as
academic—chief of the department at NYU medical school.
For no good reason, he agreed to meet with me in his office.

Short and lean, a bit over five and a half feet tall, his
energy and confidence made him seem bigger and younger
than his sixty-two years. Until I met Mailer, twenty-
two years later, I'd consider him the most confident and
assertive—and egoistic—man I'd ever known. One felt he
was always in a hurry, his schedule packed with urgent,
nonnegotiable, concrete duties, but his mind kept up with
them. He rarely paused before answering, and he had no
patience for small talk or socializing or, at times, the simplest forms of etiquette.

I hoped that he would suggest research for me, help my
work with permissions and introductions. First, however,
it seemed necessary to describe the book that had brought
me here. I summarized it briefly, doing my best to make it
seem more rational and less extreme than—in those days
anyway—it seemed to me.

Hands clasped on his desk, he was patient and attentive.
Honest too, and as always, quick to answer. "Mind-brain
stuff, right? I have to admit that sort of thing doesn't grab
me. I know some of my colleagues like to think about it,
but it's never been high on my list of priorities."

I asked if he could suggest research I might explore.

"For a book like that? I guess I'd look into rehab. Symptoms and deficits. Postsurgical patients, stroke patients, neurological disease like Parkinsonism. Alzheimer's of course. Aphasia. Amnesia. Motor deficit. Almost any sort of brain damage. Call me next week. I'll think of some names for you."

I thanked him for his time and stood to leave, but he had a question for me.

"Have you ever seen neurosurgery?"

"No."

"I'm doing an interesting case tomorrow. Why don't you come and watch?"

Offhand, a last minute thought, the invitation, as it turned out, was life changing for me. I met him next morning at six in the surgeons' locker room. Fifteen minutes later, scrubbed and dressed in the same surgical greens he wore, I was standing behind him as he removed a piece of the skull of a four-year-old boy in order to access and excise what proved to be a benign tumor in the right frontal lobe. Allowed free movement in the room, especially when Ransohoff and his assistants took a break, I leaned close enough to the striated, gelatinous flesh to see it throb and pulsate. *Real brain.* The living flesh that contained the neurons and synapses I thought of so often when I sat in zazen. As I leaned in and stared, I could not resist the thought that this was precisely the sort of tissue that made it possible for me to lean and stare, not to mention entertain the self-conscious thought I was at that moment pursuing. Was this sort of circularity a leap into the essence of the brain or a banal oversimplification, a denial of its mystery?

The procedure was done with a surgical microscope that projected an image of the child's brain on a large, wall-mounted video monitor. Since the surgical site was draped, the face covered, the child was just an object for me until, walking around the room, I saw his tiny toes curling and uncurling and was overcome with a nausea that brought me near to vomiting. I realized that such awareness did not trouble Ransohoff and the colleagues (two residents, two nurses, and an anesthesiologist) who were assisting him, but their detachment—the skill and concentration their work required, the life-and-death fact of its outcome, and the lighthearted banter they enjoyed throughout the procedure—intensified my own awareness that the child on the table was not just a lump of physical matter but an experiencing person. Moment by moment, the scene that stretched before me became more vivid and dramatic. I was so exhilarated by the light, the information and energy, and the wondrous, spectacular detail in the room that it seemed to imprint in my memory like nothing I'd known before. Later, when I hurried to record it in my notebook, it came in a rush from which nothing, I felt certain, had been excluded.

Back in the locker room, quite without reflecting on it, I asked Ransohoff if I could do a book on him. It was a reckless idea of course, but at that moment, in the wake of the OR experience, it seemed logical, exciting, and, though my novel was far from my mind just then, a happy escape from the impossible contradictions I'd left in my office.

Fortunately, Ransohoff was in a reckless state of mind himself. It so happened that he'd reached a stage in his career and in his narcissism where the idea of being followed, observed, and described by a journalist was not uninteresting to him. "Why not?" he said.

Three days later, I sent a proposal to my agent. Two weeks later, she had a response from a publisher that included the most generous advance I'd ever been offered. Neurosurgery, it seemed, had marketplace value.

Ransohoff and his staff gave me free rein of the ward and the hospital in general. It was as if they considered my book and my education their personal responsibility. I had unlimited contact with those I wanted to interview, most importantly the pre- and postsurgical patients. Aphasia, amnesia, motor deficit, paraplegia, quadriplegia—brain damage was everywhere I went throughout my long days at the hospital. Mind damage, too. Again and again, I saw that suffering and response to it were not always equated or predictable. Some patients tolerated abysmal diagnoses with patience and courage, even humor. Others went to pieces in the face of relatively minor problems.

Two floors down from the ward, on the operating floor, I saw the damage confronted, challenged, and, more often than not, averted—aneurysm, blood clot, abscess, benign and malignant tumors, epilepsy, partial and extensive lobotomy, and so on. When I wasn't in surgery, I was encouraged to investigate and learn about its attendant technology: radiology, pathology, anesthesia, and so on. Arriving early every morning and, more often than not, remaining till late at night, I followed Ransohoff and his colleagues and residents on their rounds, spent private time with nurses, social workers, residents, interns, hospital administrators, and patients. Whenever he had an unusual patient, Ransohoff made sure I was introduced, and he wouldn't let me miss anything interesting in the OR. I can't imagine that any journalist ever caught a better break than I did with him and his staff.

When I arrived at the hospital, I slipped into a white coat like those the surgeons wore. It had a name tag with my photo clipped to its breast pocket. At that instant, quite magically, it seemed, I forgot the uncertainty and abstraction that, even as a journalist, I faced at my desk. Moving through the hospital, I became an object of almost worshipful gaze from patients. Nurses and orderlies stood aside to let me pass. In effect, the identity, power, and energy that my work as a writer so often undermined was granted by my clothing, my name tag, and my relations with the staff. The moments weren't few when I shared the patients' belief in me. Often as not, when I passed through the revolving doors at the main entrance to the hospital, I felt so cleansed of anxiety and uncertainty that I assumed a different identity.

I spent six months in the hospital. When I was done, the book came in a rush. Fueled by the information and detail I'd collected in the ward and the OR, I'd never written with more ease and confidence. *Brain Surgeon: An Intimate View of His World* was finished a little more than a year after I began, published—to good reviews, a paperback sale, and publication in England—six months later, in 1979. In the whole of my career, I'd never known anything like the attention it received.

By the time the book came out, I was back in the novel that had led me to it. To my amazement, I found that its comedy had become acceptable. Accurate and true in fact. How was it possible that my experience with real brain damage had given me permission to laugh—or at least smile—at its absurdity? That such absurdity seemed existential and profound? Since my zazen practice continued and I met up with my defiant, rattling brain every time I sat, I could not give up the idea of universal brain damage, but I was able to forget, at least while at my desk, that I owed my language to my neurology. Journalism had not answered all my questions, but it had shown me how to forget them.

THOUGH UNEQUIVOCAL in his opinion of Zen, Norman was also unequivocal in his view of *Ambivalent Zen*. He gave me a very strong blurb which I used on the cover, and he recommended it to several readers, including—when she expressed an interest in studying Zen—his daughter, Maggie. About the book's most important character, Kyudo Roshi, he was however decidedly ambivalent. Three months after reading the book, he mentioned him idly, apropos of nothing, when we were headed for dinner in my car. "What's going on with this teacher of yours? He sounds like a total asshole." But one year and some months after that, he asked me about him again. "How's your teacher doing? What an amazing man he must be."

SOON AFTER ROSHI'S ARRIVAL from Japan, I receive a phone call from the secretary of a revered Tibetan lama named Dzigar Kongtrul Rinpoche. I'd met him through friends who were his students. Since I was not a student of Tibetan Buddhism, we had a relaxed, informal friendship that Rinpoche seemed to appreciate as much as I did. In his midforties at this time, he was monastically trained in northern India. He is the son and brother of other lamas and has been in the United States for a bit more than a decade. During this time, he has attracted a great number of students who, communicating and meeting often with each other, have developed a vibrant sangha. He maintains retreat and practice centers in Colorado, Vermont, Japan, and Brazil. Speaking often in public and working with students in these centers, he is frequently on the road, but he always returns to his own practice at his private retreat cabin in Colorado.

He is in New York for a teaching engagement. His secretary explains that he's just finished reading *Ambivalent Zen* and, impressed with my portrait of Roshi, would like very much to meet with him.

Roshi agrees to the meeting. A late-afternoon time is set for Rinpoche and one of his students to meet for tea with Roshi and me.

The conversation is respectful and polite but inconsequential until, near its conclusion, Rinpoche asks two favors of Roshi. First: "Would it be possible for me to remain for evening sitting?" And, second, after Roshi agrees: "Could I ask you to give me a koan?"

"Of course," says Roshi. He studies Rinpoche for a moment and then curls his hand into a fist and places it on the table between them. "What is this?" he says. The sight of his fist reminds me of Mailer's first thumb-wrestling challenge until I remember that, combined with Roshi's question, it is a classic koan—in fact it wasn't long ago that Roshi assigned it to me.

Later that evening, after zazen, Rinpoche and I head for Chinatown, where he wants to visit a favorite restaurant. It is always a privilege to be with him, but I've never felt it more than tonight. Once again, zazen has brought me to vivid awareness of the present moment and the thought that my brain seems opposed to it. After my time at the hospital, I've become very resistant to associating brain damage with zazen or for that matter anything else, but the present-tense experience I came to on my cushion makes resistance difficult. Isn't the present moment free of time altogether? Isn't time itself a neurological function? How can anyone who practices sitting meditation avoid suspicion of the brain? But how be surprised that a practice that generates such impossible thought—and thought about it!—leaves me so frightened and destabilized?

As we walk toward Chinatown, Rinpoche praises the quiet of the zendo and the energy he'd felt in our zazen. I agree. The atmosphere in the zendo is always powerful when Roshi is in the room, but tonight, perhaps because of Rinpoche's presence, it had seemed even more so.

"Yes," I say, "it was quiet all right. But I have to admit it made me very uncomfortable. It seems to me sometimes that my brain can't tolerate where the practice takes me. Sometimes, zazen seems a sort of drug, like nitrous oxide or cocaine. It takes you to states of mind you can't sustain and later, when you come down from them, can't bear to let go of."

Rinpoche laughs. "I wish I could say I'm not familiar with that problem, but I know it well. It's hard to imagine that anyone who comes to dharma practice with an intelligent, open mind would not come up against this problem."

"Do you think it's as common in Tibetan practice as it is in Zen?"

"Sure it is. I'm not exactly an expert in Zen, but nothing I know about it conflicts with our path. It's true perhaps that you place more emphasis on sitting than we do, but no matter what practice we do, our paths are a means of breaking through ego and self-cherishing, finding our way to altruism and compassion, what we call *bodhichitta*, or 'loving-kindness.' What are we doing but opening our hearts, finding a way to help others, relieve suffering in all sentient beings? Perhaps my words are different from Roshi's, but I don't think our goals are different."

Nearing Chinatown, we walk in silence for the last few blocks. As always when I am with Rinpoche or, for that matter, any dharma teacher, I am swept with feelings of devotion and gratitude, amazed at the karma that has brought me connection with them. These are people, after all, who have given their lives to the practice, who embody the lineage that goes back to Shakyamuni Buddha. The practice is part-time for me, a brief detour from my busy, distracted, conventional life. For people like Rinpoche and Roshi, it is full-time, total sacrifice, a disciplined stand against the pleasures and escapes of the phenomenal world. Is it the "part-time" nature of my practice that makes it so often confusing for me?

The entrance to the restaurant is at the top of a short stairway from the street. As we reach the door, I say, "Well, whatever our path, whichever practice we choose, it all comes down to the present moment, doesn't it? Everything else is an illusion."

"Of course," says Rinpoche. "But the present moment is an illusion too."

FOUR

For years, as homage, I'd sent Beckett, care of his publisher, everything I published. I had no connection or introduction to him. With a separate letter to introduce it, I sent him a copy of *Brain Surgeon* after it came out in 1979. Of course I'd never had a response from him, and this being journalism, a kind of writing I imagined he abjured, I thought my chances less than ever.

Two weeks later, I opened my mailbox to find his answer, in an envelope with no return address. His handwriting was close to illegible—very small, very precise, almost like calligraphy—but after several moments, I was able to decipher it.

> Dear Mr. Shainberg
>
> I received and read your book before your letter reached me. It impressed me strongly. I read it too fast and shall read it again. Mere decay is a paltry affair beside the calamities you describe. It is all I can speak of. And the ever acuter awareness of it. And the preposterous conviction, formed long ago, that here in the end is the last & by far best chance for a writer. Gaping into his synaptic chasms. Forgive such poor private response to your book & letter. I am a poor hand at this form of communication.
>
> With all good wishes for yr. future work,
> yrs very cordially
> Sam Beckett

Stunned with disbelief, I wrote to thank him and, riding the wave of my excitement, asked if I could one day meet him directly. Again I didn't expect an answer and again I was wrong. He wrote that he'd be pleased to see me if and when our paths cross, adding, "Any chance you'll be in Europe soon?"

As it happened, the British version of *Brain Surgeon* was scheduled to be published a few months later, and I was set to do publicity in London. Amazingly enough, Beckett wrote that his schedule would take him to London at the same time for rehearsals of a production of *Endgame* that he himself would direct.

Thus it was that a few months later, a day after I arrived in London, sleeping off my jet lag in the early afternoon, the phone rang in my London hotel room.

"Hello, Mr. Shainberg. Sam Beckett here."

He was cordial on the phone and even more cordial later that day when, at his invitation, I met him at his hotel. I was seriously nervous, but the first surprise on meeting him was the speed with which—greeting me, for all the world, as if honored by my visit—he put me at my ease.

This was London's Hyde Park Hotel. A small, comfortable room with a single bed, an upholstered easy chair, and a dressing table with a small upholstered bench in front of it. No sign of its occupant except a brown corduroy jacket on the bed, a carry-on bag in the corner, and, on the dressing table, a notebook, several small medicine bottles, and four books. From across the room I could see Dante and, just beneath him, *Endgame*, in the same softcover edition I had brought with me and reread on the plane coming over. Beckett directed me to the easy chair, poured Irish whiskeys for both of us, took a seat on a corner of the bed, and plied me with questions: How was my flight from New York? How long will I be in London? How is my book doing?

Do I still see the surgeons I wrote about? What about the patients? How are they doing now?

His Irish accent was pronounced and musical. This was as close to small talk as I'd ever get with him. I was not so calm that I did not fix with obsession on the iconic face I knew so well from his book jackets. I felt a sort of disbelief when I asked him, as I'd ask most any old-friend-writer I saw all the time, "How's your work going?"

Though I asked casually, the question was anything but trivial to him. A long pause ensued. He closed his eyes for a moment and, in a gesture I'd soon learn was habitual with him, a sign that he'd sunk into concentration, put his long middle finger over the space between his nose and upper lip. Later on, when we established a correspondence, I'd often imagine him thinking like this just before he wrote me. This was not, of course, because our friendship was remarkably intimate but because, on subjects that were important to him, he never took it for granted that he'd have another chance with them.

"You know, I always thought old age would be a writer's best chance. Whenever I read the late work of Goethe or W. B. Yeats, I had the impertinence to identify with it. Now—my memory's gone. All the old fluency has disappeared. I don't write a single sentence without saying to myself, 'It's a lie!' So I know I was right. It's the best chance I've ever had."

The silence between us was palpable. His concentration seemed to evoke the same in me.

"It's a paradox," he continued, "but with old age, the more the possibilities diminish, the better chance you have. With diminished concentration, loss of memory, obscured intelligence—what you, I suspect, would call 'brain damage'—the more chance there is for saying something closest to what one really is. Even though everything seems inexpressible, there remains the need to express. A child needs to make a sand castle even though it makes no sense to him. In old age, with only a few grains of sand, one has the greatest possibility."

Seventy-four years old, he looked frail that night, a lot more gaunt than his photos had led me to expect. For a man who had once called writing "disimproving the silence" and had gone through periods of debilitating depression, especially in his thirties, he had been writing fairly steadily since his early twenties, publishing twelve novels, sixteen plays, fourteen radio plays, a film script, and a remarkable book of criticism, on Proust, when he was twenty-five. Though shy and slow to trust, he was also, as I was already discovering, relaxed and happy in conversation once issues of trust were resolved. It was ten years since he'd been awarded the Nobel Prize and thirty-four since a cathartic experience had led to a major redirection in his work, producing the novels that had so encouraged my Zen practice.

Later that evening, I mentioned how much those novels had meant to me. "Yes," he said, sighing. "They were crucial for me as well." Closing his eyes, he disappeared behind his hand again. Then he repeated to me, as if discovering it for the first time, a story that, like anyone who knew the Beckett literature, I knew very well myself.

"When I returned to Dublin after the war, I found that my mother had contracted Parkinson's disease. Her face was a mask, completely unrecognizable. Looking at her, I had the sudden realization that all the work I'd done before was on the wrong track. I guess you'd have to call it a revelation. Strong word, I know, but so it was. I simply understood that there was no sense adding to the store of information, gathering knowledge. The whole attempt at knowledge, it seemed to me, had come to nothing. It was all haywire. What I had to do was investigate not-knowing, not-perceiving, the whole world of incompleteness."

In the wake of this insight, writing in French—"Perhaps because French is not my mother tongue, because I had no facility in it, no spontaneity"—while still in his mother's house, he had begun *Molloy*. Its first line—"I am in my mother's room"—commenced what was to be the most prolific period of his life. Within the first three paragraphs of his chronicle, Molloy says "I don't know" six times, "perhaps" and "I've forgotten" twice, and "I don't understand" once. He doesn't know how he came to be in his mother's room, he doesn't know how to write anymore, and he doesn't know why he writes when he manages to do so. He doesn't know whether his mother was dead when he came to her room or died later, and he doesn't know whether or not he has a son. In other words, he is not much different from any other writer in the anxiety of composition—considering the alternative roads offered up by his imagination and memory, trying to discern a theme amid the chaos of information offered by his brain, testing his language to see what sort of relief it can offer.

Molloy and his creator were joined from the start, and the latter—unlike most other writers, who had been taught, even if they were writing about their own ignorance and uncertainty, that the strength of their work consisted in their ability to pretend otherwise—is saying "I don't know" with every word he utters. The whole of his narrative is therefore time-dependent, neurologically and psychologically suspect, and contingent upon the fluctuations of the narrator's mind. And since knowledge, by definition, requires a subject and an object, a knower and a known, two points separated on the temporal continuum, Beckett's "I don't know" short-circuited the fundamental dualism from which most narrative before him had been derived. If two points cannot be separated on this continuum, what is left? No time, only the present moment. And if you must speak in the present, using words, which are by definition object-dependent, how do you do so? Finally, what is left to know if knowledge itself has been discredited? Without an object, what will words describe or subjugate? If subject and object are joined, how can there be hope or order or memory? What is hoped for, what is ordered, what is remembered? What is self if knower and known are not separated by self-consciousness?

How could one be surprised that, though they speak of Joyce, Proust, and other masters in terms of genius, many writers speak of Beckett in terms of courage? One almost has to be a writer to know what courage it takes to stand so naked before one's reader—or, more important, before oneself. To relinquish the protection offered by detachment from the narrative, the security and order that, in all likelihood, were what drew one to writing in the first place. How could I be surprised that Beckett's work and Zen seemed deeply intertwined to me? That the practice of sitting, following the breath, seemed to take me to the place and time from which his work derived?

When I was about to leave that evening, he asked me about my own work. "What are you doing these days?"

I told him about the novel, now called *Memories of Amnesia*, that had inspired and then paralyzed me and finally led me to the neurosurgeons. I did not mention that of all my work, it was the book most influenced by him. After *Brain Surgeon*, I'd returned to it, finding it ventilated, freed of its conceptualizations, and, to my surprise, more comic than anything I'd written before. I told him I'd brought the manuscript with me, hoping against hope that he'd look at it. As a matter of fact, had it right here in my briefcase.

"I'd be happy to read it," he said.

I left it with him. The next day, as we rode in a taxi to the theater, he told me—to my amazement—that he'd read it. My rush of excitement was cut short by the pained, apologetic look on his face. "I'm sorry—in my view, it doesn't work," he said. "It's not your voice. It's just not you." And then, with a single, sad, conclusive diagnosis, he told me why I did not have to suffer as he did. "Your line," he said, "is witnessing."

Arriving at the theater, he was clearly in good spirits. Away from his desk, he was exploring, in *Endgame*, a work that, written thirty years before, remained among his favorites. Still engaged with the text, he continued to edit it, making changes as the rehearsals progressed. The American group, called the San Quentin Drama Workshop (because they had discovered his work, through a visiting production of *Waiting for Godot*, while inmates at San Quentin), was particularly close to his heart, and here in London, he was accessible to a close-knit group of friends and admirers that collected so often when he was working there. It included three writers with Beckett books in progress, two editors who published him and one who wanted to, and an impressive collection of Beckett freaks who had learned of his presence through the grapevine. A woman in her late sixties came to ask if Beckett minded that she'd named her dog after him. ("Don't worry about me. What about the dog?") A wild-eyed madman from Scotland brought flowers and gifts for Beckett and everyone in the cast, as well as a four-page letter entitled "Beckett's Cancer, Part Three," which begged him to accept the gifts as a "sincere token of my deep and long-suffering love for you," while remembering that "I also hold a profound and comprehensive loathing for you, in response to all the terrible corruption and suffering which you have seen fit to inflict upon my entirely innocent personality."

At the time of his visit with his mother, Beckett was thirty-nine years old, which is to say, the same age as Krapp—the sole character in *Krapp's Last Tape*—who deals with a revelation almost the same as Beckett's in his tape-recorded journals and ends by rejecting it: "What a fool I was to take that for a vision!" That evening, however, as we sat in his hotel room, there was no rejection in Beckett's mind. In the three years that followed his breakthrough, he told me, he'd written *Molloy, Malone Dies, The Unnamable, Stories and Texts for Nothing,* and—in three months, with almost no revision of his first draft—*Waiting for Godot.* The last, he said, was "pure recreation." The novels, especially *The Unnamable*, had taken him to a point where there were no limits, and *Godot* was a conscious attempt to reestablish them. His explanation reminded me of the freedom I found in journalism. "I wanted walls I could touch, rules I had to follow." I asked if his initial revelation—the understanding, as he'd put it, that all his previous work had been a lie— had depressed him. "No, I was very excited! There was no effort in the writing. I worked all day and went out to the cafés at night."

He was visibly excited by the memory, but it wasn't long before his mood shifted. The contrast between the days he'd remembered and the difficulty he was having now— "racking my brain," as he put it, "to see if I can go a little farther"—was almost unbearable. He sighed and covered his eyes with his hand. "If only it could be like that again!"

So this was the other side of his equation, one that I, like many of his admirers, had a tendency to forget. The enthusiasm he often expressed for his diminishments did not protect him from the pain those diminishments caused. Why should he miss such painful work when it deserted him? It was so easy to be inspired by the way he embraced his ignorance and absurdity, so hard to remember that when he did so, he wasn't posturing or for that matter "writing"—that what kept his comedy alive was the pain and despair and impotence from which it was won. The sincerity of writers who work with pain and impotence is threatened by the vitality the work itself engenders, but Beckett somehow thrived in this equation. He had never allowed his work to displace his experience. Though he'd often said that his real work began when he "gave up hope for meaning," he hated hopelessness and longed for meaning as much as anyone who'd never read *Molloy* or seen *Endgame*.

One of our less happy exchanges would occur because of my tendency to forget this. It was in 1980, on a cold rainy morning in Paris, when he was talking, yet again, about the difficulties he was having in his work. "These days, I don't know what I'm doing. I can't even bring myself to open the exercise book. My hand goes out to it, then draws back as if on its own!" Though he'd often spoken like this, sounding less like a man who'd been writing for almost sixty years than one who'd just begun, he was unusually depressed that morning, and the more he talked, the more depressed I became myself. No question about it, one had to have a powerful equanimity to remain untouched by his grief. The more I listened to him, the more it occurred to me that he sounded exactly like Molloy. Who else could speak with such authority about paralysis and bewilderment—a condition, in other words, which was antithetical to authority itself? Finally, I could not resist passing my thought along to him.

"If I had to choose my favorite Beckett line," I said, "it would be Molloy's 'If there's one question I dread, to which I've never been able to invent a satisfactory reply, it's 'What are you doing?'"

So complete was my excitement with this resolution that I expected him to share it. Why not? It seemed to me that, in words of his own invention, I'd come upon the perfect antidote to his despair. It took but a single glance from him—the only anger I ever saw in his eyes—to show me how naïve I'd been, how silly to think that Molloy would offer him the giddy freedom he had so often offered me. "Yes," Beckett muttered, "that's my line, isn't it?" Not for him the pleasures of Beckett.

As Henry James once said, "My job is to write those little things, not read them."

As usual, Roshi's New York visit will climax with a seven-day retreat, a *sesshin*, in our small zendo in Soho. About twenty of us will bring sleeping bags, towels, toiletries, and other necessities, arriving on a Friday evening and remaining until lunch the following Friday. We'll sleep on the floor, sleeping bags arranged about six inches apart, earplugs tight to protect us from our fellow students' snoring. If we like, we can use our small round cushions, called *zafus*, for pillows, but since Roshi believes that this can make you (yes, he says it often) insane, we've been warned to enclose them in pillow cases.

Rarely leaving the zendo except for short walks in the neighborhood, we'll avoid all but essential speech, eat all meals in silence on our cushions, sit nine hours a day or more if we choose to continue during breaks or (as some students do) overnight, chant an extensive liturgy that mixes English, Sino-Japanese, and Pali, listen to one of Roshi's talks every day, and meet with him every other day for private interview. Gradually, we'll come to feel that there is no separation between us, understand again and again, as if for the first time, why the word *sesshin* means "one mind."

Though space requirements, obviously, force changes and adaptations, the form and schedule and principle of sesshin have remained essentially the same since Zen, as Ch'an Buddhism, developed in third-century China and moved on to Japan and the Western world over time. What we'll do is not a whole lot different from what Chinese practitioners did over a millennium ago.

Though I've done these retreats for more than thirty years—including with several other teachers before I met Roshi—the week before one begins is sadly familiar in its difficulty. Of course, it's major separation anxiety I face. Hard to imagine that one would ever find a more perfect focus for it. As I prepare to leave—organizing books and papers, setting up vacation messages on email and answering machine and so forth—I am sleeping poorly, overeating, and seriously constipated. How is it possible that after all these years, when I've proved to myself again and again that I not only survive these retreats but come out of them quieter, stronger, and happier, I remain so frightened of them? I explore it all in my journal, explaining it to myself as carefully as I can, but knowledge brings no purchase on this slope. The moments aren't few when the whole idea of sesshin seems like either a weakness I'm indulging or an act of masochism. If the past is any guide, I'll decide more than once during this week to cancel altogether.

Organizing files and books is never easy for me, but thanks to my endless Mailer-Beckett book, it's harder this time than ever. I've written a good part of it, but I'm haunted by its incompleteness and the fact that I'm still writing on instinct, still not sure why the four-person quadrangle of Roshi and me and Mailer and Beckett has haunted me for years. Why have I taken on the weight of two characters who occupy so much space in literary history? Is it enough that they were my friends? That they are polar opposites on the literary spectrum? That my own mind seems to contain their polarities? That Zen and Roshi seem to unite them? These questions have nagged me for years, and in the week before sesshin, as I look toward a break from writing itself, they become more and more desperate and disturbing.

I try to take my ambivalence as a metaphor of my subject, but how can I deny that it seems another form of constipation?

THE NEXT TIME I saw Beckett, in Paris, I found him in very good spirits. He said he was exploring a new medium. He'd long been open to such exploration, writing radio plays, an opera, using a tape recorder in *Krapp's Last Tape*, and exploring cinema with *Film*, the silent film he'd made in New York City with Buster Keaton. What he had in mind now, he said, was "a crazy invention for TV."

He took a small notebook from his pocket and showed me a drawing in pencil. It wasn't easy to understand. The principal form was a quadrangle with the letters *A, B, C,* and *D* at the corners. Dotted lines connected each letter, arrows ran along the perimeter, and lines went to the center, which was marked with an X. The piece was called "Quad," he said. It had begun with a mime he'd tried to write more than fifteen years earlier. He explained that he meant it to be a nonverbal piece for four dancers, each wearing hooded robes, with a percussive accompaniment. "I want to bring them in fast, have them walk around the perimeter, each of them half the quadrangle, then along the diagonal. All must avoid the center. It's a danger zone."

Eventually titled *Quadrat I & II*, this twelve-minute piece would be brought to the screen in 1982, when Beckett was seventy-five years old. He'd never been a "popular" writer, of course, but it may have been, of all his works, the least noted or discussed. Manic, hypnotic, and mysteriously comic, it's as close as he ever got to his bottom line. As Graley Herren wrote of it in the *Journal of Dramatic Theory and Criticism*, "He *does* seem to be boring one hole after another into language in the teleplays until, by the time he produces *Quadrat I & II* in 1982, he is left with all hole and no language."*

The hole would not remain empty for long. Soon after *Quad* was complete, he wrote three brief paragraphs of a new piece of prose, called *Better Worse* in its early drafts and *Worstward Ho* when it appeared in 1982. It began with eight sentences, the last of which is one of his most famous.

"All before. Nothing else ever. Ever tried. Ever failed. No matter. Try again. Fail again. Fail better."

Of this work, his biographer James Knowlson would write, "In order to fail better, the strategy Beckett adapted was to strive for the worst." But as always, Beckett never denied the irony of his project, using words to probe the realm that is beyond them. "The language," writes Knowlson, "is

---

*Graley Herren, "Samuel Beckett's *Quad*: Pacing to Byzantium," *Journal of Dramatic Theory and Criticism* 15, no. 1 (Fall 2000): 44.

almost heroic in its mad determination to go on. The void cannot be conquered, but it can still be described, especially when part of the description is the writer's inability to describe it."*

Sᴇssʜɪɴ ʙᴇɢɪɴs on Friday evening. After lunch, I take my dog to the kennel where she'll board while I'm away. She's six years old, a white, midsized Labradoodle named Ruby. Beautiful and soulful, I consider her the quintessential dog, and I suspect that most people who know me consider that I'm the quintessential dog owner. Though I've learned not to talk about her too much, she is a fixture in my thoughts. The simplest, most obvious thing about her—that she lives entirely in the present moment—can strike me, again and again, as a miracle I'm seeing for the first time, the very essence of Zen.

A few days after I got her, I had dinner with Mailer. Though I resisted the temptation to celebrate her too much, I brought a picture to show him.

"She's very beautiful," he said. "What's the mix?"

"Lab and poodle."

"Wonderful combination, no? I used to have a poodle."

*James Knowlson, *Damned to Fame: The Life of Samuel Beckett* (New York: Simon & Schuster, 1996), 593–94.

"I know," I said. "Named Tibo, right?"

"How do you know that?"

"I read about him in the Manso biography."*

"Oh, that horseshit. You mustn't trust anything Manso says. Some of the book is true of course, but most of it is distortion and exaggeration."

He sipped his drink. "Tibo was a great dog—beautiful, powerful, incredibly intelligent—but there was one thing that traumatized him."

"What was that?"

"That he couldn't speak English. You could see his yearning when you looked in his eyes. I always thought that if I were a better writer I could have taught him."

AT THAT TIME, he was working with Lennon on the massive job of his letter collection and immensely enjoying, he said, the chance to revisit emotions he'd left behind. Over dinner one night, he told me about feelings close to joy that had been evoked by rereading his letters with William Buckley—correspondence that had varied between extremes of warm friendship and vicious insult. Nothing

---

*Peter Manso, *Mailer: His Life and Times* (New York: Washington Square Press, 1985).

pleased him so much, he said, as "remembering how vicious I could be."

The memory took him to fistfights in the dark days of his youth, the inclination toward head butting that had preceded his confrontation with Gore Vidal on the *Dick Cavett Show*, and, less happily, the night when he stabbed his second wife.

"It's painful to think of that, but I have to admit it's great to realize that I wasn't always a nice guy. I remember especially a night in Edinburgh, drinking with a small group of people at the end of a conference. It was a great time for me because I'd met Henry Miller and William Burroughs there. Among those in our party was a translator who was unbearably maudlin, complaining at great length about some hoodlums who'd mugged him that afternoon. 'How can human beings treat each other like this?' That sort of thing. He went on and on about it till I couldn't stand it anymore. I took him by the lapels and threw him down the stairs. 'I'll show you how human beings can treat each other,' I said. Before I let go of him, he gave me a look I treasure to this day. I knew I'd never again have to pretend I'm nicer than I am."

In addition to the letters, he was working on a collection of essays and selections from his previous work, which was meant to be an anthology of advice on the writing profession. What this book needed, he said one night, was a chapter on Beckett. "Why don't you come over and interview me about him? I think that might lead to something good."

Thus it was that a few days later—fifteen years after I asked Beckett if he'd ever read Mailer and he said, "Yes—he's a bit copious for me."—I placed a recorder between Norman and me and asked, "How much Beckett have you read?"

"Not much. A few of the plays but not the novels."

The ensuing interview lasted about ninety minutes. He did not use it verbatim in the book but summarized it in the resulting chapter. Though he began by acknowledging that *Waiting for Godot* had "dimension, resonance, vibrancy," he was probing about its author's differences from him. They centered on "nothingness." Beckett understood, he wrote, that nothingness was "half of life," but unlike most writers, for whom it was "anathema," he meant to "dwell" on it. He granted that Beckett is "lively and witty as he travels into these subtly fetid caves of virtual non-existence," but asserted that he differed from him in that "I always saw such states as the price you pay in order to command a grasp of existence, of being."*

Though the distinction struck me as awkward at first, I came to realize that it was precisely here, in Mailer's

*Norman Mailer, *The Spooky Art: Thoughts on Writing* (New York: Random House, 2003), 164.

determination to "command a grasp of existence," that he and Beckett diverged. Beckett, after all, had announced early on in his career that his work was about "exploiting impotence." The act of "exploiting" is a challenge to impotence. Since true impotence does not allow for it, this was Beckett's paradox. It was also, I realized, where the contrast between him and Mailer lay. Beckett's work was a vivid demonstration of his singular ability to exploit and constantly reaffirm his impotence. By contrast, a writer like Mailer, who meant to "command a grasp of existence," was essentially driven to transcend any impotence that afflicted him. Indeed, the effort to "command a grasp of existence" was not a bad summary for the fierce resolve and energy that had driven Mailer's career.

While the difference between him and Beckett made them, in my view, polar opposites as writers, it was ironic. Who could deny the energy and courage—in other words, the potency—which Beckett's *exploitation* of impotence had required? How else had he managed the fierce confrontation with nothingness which Mailer pointed out? And how could Mailer have managed the brilliant detachment of books like *Armies of the Night* or *Executioner's Song* without facing his own futility and insufficiency—the nothingness, and perhaps the impotence, he'd not been able to escape? While Beckett found Mailer "too copious" and Mailer begrudged Beckett's determination to "stay in noth-

ingness," they'd both managed to hang on for decades in the
close-to-impossible paths they'd chosen. And even though
my talent was not close to theirs, and my vision rooted in
a spiritual practice which neither could comprehend, both
had saved me often when my own surges of impotence and
contradiction exceeded my ability to exploit them.

FIVE

'

AFTER LEAVING RUBY at the kennel, I return home and complete my packing: the robe I'll wear for sitting, pillowcase to cover my cushion, towel, ear plugs, the nest of black lacquer bowls we use when—in silence, of course—we eat together at our cushions. Finally, backpack and sleeping bag on my shoulder, heading for the door, I pause, as I do every time I head out for sesshin, to reread a letter pinned to the bulletin board over my desk. It's Beckett's reply to a note I wrote him five years ago—"Dear Sam: Please tell me what it is about looking at a wall which makes writing seem obsolete."—after I returned from a sesshin like the one to which I'm headed now.

Dear Larry,

When I look at walls, I begin to see the writing, from which even my own is a relief.

Solitude is paradise.

Best/Sam

O<small>NE NIGHT DURING DINNER</small>, I interrupted an attack on Zen that Norman had mounted *even before* we sat down and continued while we were waiting for our drinks: "You know your problem? You confuse nothingness with emptiness."

"What's the difference?" he said.

"Nothingness is form."

"What isn't form?"

"Emptiness."

"And emptiness? How would you define it?"

"I don't know. One teacher I know, Bernie Glassman, said that while most people think it means absence of content, what it really means is absence of description."

"Description?" Mailer nodded, sipping his drink again. The expression on his face was uncharacteristically quizzical. "That makes sense. I've got to take a piss. Let's talk about it when I get back."

By the time he got back, I'd had a bit more vodka, and he had other things on his mind. Football, as I recall. Which interested me, as it happened, no less than it did him. We never pursued the definition of emptiness I'd offered him, but as I'd see after his death, when I read his last book, the question of emptiness and nothingness never ceased to obsess him. Eventually, it found its way into his last book, but as I'd see when I read it, my teacher's definition had been translated into Mailer language and Mailer metaphor— *Mailer description*—and he had it, in my view, all wrong. Not many subjects escaped the force of his energy and intelligence, but the degree to which he took possession of them was often costly and distorting. Of all the discussions we failed to complete, this may have been the most important. It's certainly the one that makes me saddest.

ON THE FIRST NIGHT of sesshin, the short walk from my apartment to the zendo is a convoluted and intimidating odyssey. Tonight it seems worse than ever. Two days from now, maybe tomorrow, the zendo will seem a paradisaical escape from the urban madness that surrounds me on this sidewalk, but right now I feel as if headed for a black hole.

I'm early at the zendo, but ten or twelve of the twenty people who'll participate in sesshin are already milling about in the dressing room. I know most of them well. It's a co-ed group with ages ranging from forty to late seventies. Two physicians, a social worker, a psychiatrist, a performance artist, a seventy-year-old photographer who once lived at Dai Bosatsu—the monastery that Soen Roshi founded in the Catskills—a stock broker who began practice at least thirty years ago with Suzuki Roshi in California, Kazuko of course, and Amnon, who runs his own gardening business in New Jersey. I'm glad to see them and grateful to know they'll share this voyage with me, but my breath is short, and my anxiety edges toward claustrophobia as we change into the clothes we'll use for zazen. Most of us wear the brown robes that Roshi, after choosing the cloth, arranged to have sewn for us twenty-five years ago, in the early days of the zendo, but some, from other zendos, wear grey or black robes or loose-fitting skirts or pants that would be at home on the street or in the gym.

Entering the zendo, we find Roshi on his cushion next to the altar. He likes to be there ten or fifteen minutes before we arrive. Despite his eighty-year-old legs, he sits in full lotus, gazing toward the floor in front of him. As usual, he's set out our cushions in the alignment he's always favored—six feet from the wall, six inches apart, ten each in parallel rows perpendicular to the altar. The cushions are made of foam rubber. He bought them himself, chose the brown fabric with which they're covered, arranged for their upholstery and, until he returned to Japan, removed the covers once a year, took them to a dry cleaner, and picked them up himself. Though one or several of us usually volunteered to help, he seemed to enjoy the not-easy task of fitting the rubber into the cloth of the forty cushions we maintain for members and visitors. Each of the round, brown zafus has a small hook of cloth for use as a handle, and—with key chains, ribbons, shoelaces, or even carefully sewn initials—those of us who use the same cushion all the time have marked it to identify the cushion as our own. Zafus differ in height, width, and resilience, and given the degree to which our backs, groins, and legs depend on them, our connection to them can seem a kind of intimacy.

A few minutes later, at 7:00 p.m. exactly, Roshi strikes two wooden sticks (*hyōshigi*) together and then lifts a small bronze bell from an upholstered cushion and strikes it three times. The diminishing reverberations of this bell are meant to be a gentle transition to the absolute silence in which we sit. It has often worked that way for me in the past, but tonight, amid the increasing momentum and fragmentation of my thoughts, the gently fading sound of the bell only reminds me once again that I'm offering myself up to the capricious chatter of my brain.

I sit erect on my cushion, push my head toward the ceiling, try my best, in vain, to ignore the thought that I'll be here for seven days. Show me anything crueler, at moments like this, than the idea of duration. Flashes of terror continue until I remember an exchange I had with Roshi—on a day when he had spoken about the inescapable fact of suffering in the phenomenal world.*

"Isn't Buddhism about healing pain and suffering?"

"Of course it is."

"Well, how does it happen? How does a Buddhist heal the pain of suffering?"

"He takes it."

The memory doesn't bring me peace, but it turns me in its direction. With each breath, I seem to inhale and exhale my anxiety. If it doesn't diminish, at least it becomes familiar. After all, I can't go anywhere, and within a few minutes I don't want to. For a few moments at least, Zen seems magical, all-powerful, supreme in its wisdom and lucidity—but after all, there's a long way to go, and ideas like this make it longer.

The book is haunting me. Have I really persisted with this hopeless project? Through all these years, all this ambition and self-deception? Even if I manage it, who will

---

*Lawrence Shainberg, *Ambivalent Zen: One Man's Adventures on the Dharma Path* (New York: Vintage Books, 1995).

read it? Who reads anything these days? What is writing anyway but another form of brain damage? What if not disrupted neurology made me add Mailer's and Beckett's pathologies to my own? The more I try to follow my breath, the more persistent the chatter becomes.

Thirty minutes later, Roshi rings the bell and strikes his sticks again. We stand and bow to each other, turn to our left, and, with hands folded at low-belly level, circle the zendo three times. Our meditation, of course, is meant to continue as we walk. Roshi has more than once admonished us to put our minds in our feet. As we near the end of our third circumambulation, he strikes his sticks again, and we stop at our cushions, facing each other with hands together just below our chins in the position called *gassho*. Finally, he rings the bell once more, and we bow to each other and take our seats again.

Rain begins a few minutes later. We have an air conditioner in the window, and it amplifies the sound. In the silence of the zendo, it mesmerizes. All at once, I'm safe and confident, happy to be here and, because manic follows quickly on depression, exploding with confidence. For a good thirty seconds. Enough at least to know why I'm here. Why I need to be here. Why I've been here for years. Then a rebound to anxiety—thoughts of my book in humiliating detail. Nothing threatens the cortical brain like meditation, and the brain, I'm convinced, responds with agitation and cruel, incessant noise. How better to increase its velocity than confining oneself to this cushion, this breath, this one, and this one? I straighten my back, remind myself to breathe with my whole body. Posture and deep breathing would surely lead to focus and concentration if I did not expect them to do so.

As the third sitting begins, I arrive here at last. Say what you will about Zen, it is not passive before the brain, and the brain is not immune to it. I am discovering once again that the quiet mind has no thought of neurology. Each breath brings me closer to the radical freedom Zen offers—*things as they are*—but I've still got a long way to go. Things as they are, after all, is shadowed by "things as they are." How many times in the course of this week will I conclude that self-consciousness is brain damage? I'm feeling slightly more confident of surviving this ordeal, but I can't deny that these first ninety minutes have left me feeling weak and depressed, pathetic in fact, and worst of all, because after all I've got a huge Zen ego, ashamed that I'm so far behind where I want to be.

In other words, sesshin is proceeding normally. I suspect that every one of the twenty of us is enduring similar vacillations. Buddhists have done this for twenty-five hundred years, but the human brain has continued to evolve, the quantity of neurons and synapses and the complexity of neurochemistry expanding without cease and—in my view—generating, in exact proportion to such increase, the need for this sort of practice. How can one doubt that everyone in this room takes off and crashes again and again? That all of us, knowing this, grow closer to each other? Now and again, there seem to be no boundaries between us, no brain not dwarfed by the mind we share.

$\mathcal{N}$EW YORK MAGAZINE published an excerpt of *On God* two days before Mailer died, when he was in the hospital with a breathing tube in his mouth. He'd had a successful pulmonary surgery a few days before but then contracted pneumonia. When Larry Schiller—an old friend and collaborator*—showed him a copy of the magazine, he managed half a smile. His mood after all was not entirely negative. Mike Lennon would report that Mailer had told him that morning that he'd had a dream the night before in which he was God and Schiller the devil, and they made a pact to rid the world of technology. He was also engaged in a happy flirtation with a young nurse who had literary ambition. Before his surgery, she'd sought his advice on a story she was writing, and he'd promised to read it for her.

*Schiller collaborated with Mailer on *The Executioner's Song, Oswald's Tale*, and several television projects.

Standing on the other side of the bed, I watched as Schiller presented him with the magazine. This would be the last time I saw him. I had arrived awhile before Schiller, so I had a few minutes alone with Mailer and during that precious silence received from him a last note scrawled on a notebook—"Larry OK"—with the *K* descending pathetically toward the bottom of the page.

The magazine had his picture on the cover, a head shot with white hair flowing. "Mailer on God," read the headline. I'd not read the book, but when I did, I found that one section began with Lennon asking about Mailer's view of Buddhism. His answer included what seemed to be a reference to the night when, during dinner at Michael Shay's, he'd pressed me for a definition of emptiness. Even though the definition I offered—that emptiness is not the absence of content but the absence of description—had intrigued him when he heard it, he seemed to have forgotten it. Speaking to Lennon, he said that the difficulty he'd always had with Buddhism was nirvana.* Ignoring the fact that Buddhists equate nirvana with emptiness, and that, as I'd been at pains to remind him, emptiness and nothingness were not synonymous, Mailer equated nirvana with "nothingness" and

---

*His memory of our discussion might have been compromised by the fact that this conversation occurred during the last years of his life, when he was weakened and forgetful.

proceeded to take the aggressive anti-nothingness position he'd taken so often with me and, for that matter, when I interviewed him about Beckett: "I remember talking to a friend of mine who is a good Buddhist, and I soon fell into a polite rage. 'You Buddhists always talk about nothingness, at how to arrive at nothingness. . . . You're not really talking about nothingness. Nothingness is an awful state! It's so empty a state!"*

Nothing I'd said, and for that matter, nothing about Buddhism, implied a desire to "arrive at nothingness." In fact, I'd tried more than once to explain to him the essential Buddhist view of desire. It is the root of suffering, and nirvana, in effect, is freedom from it and thus acceptance of the present moment, things as they are. Freedom, in other words, from the dualistic mind, which creates and sustains desire by separating subject and object. "The first mark of enlightenment," the Buddha said, "is the ability to be content."

Anyone who knew Norman Mailer would know that such a view was anathema to him, but they'd also know that such anathema was not uncomplicated. Desire was his engine, and while he protected it against ideas that threatened it, his efforts were almost as ironic as Beckett's.

*Norman Mailer with J. Michael Lennon, *On God: An Uncommon Conversation* (New York: Random House, 2007), 200.

For all his objection to Buddhism, his life was marked with characteristics—spontaneity and awareness, generosity as a friend, and of course the energy, curiosity, and enthusiasm which had fueled his work—that were not, I'd argue, inconsistent with Buddhism. Like Beckett, his work was rooted in paradox and fierce intellectual honesty. All his life he'd been at pains to note his own contradictions, and it seemed to me that in this conversation he was addressing himself as much as his "Buddhist friend." What Buddhists were "really talking about," he said, was "the ineffable." Wasn't this—for all his passionate arguments with Buddhism—what he was really talking about himself?

I felt a great range of disappointment as I read these lines. Disappointed with Mailer because, as it seemed to me, they showed no understanding of Buddhism, and disappointed with myself because it was obvious that, despite our many conversations on the subject, I'd failed to reach him. Surely this indicated an insufficiency on my side as well as his. It was hard for me to believe that I was not the "Buddhist friend" he spoke of, that the conversation he described was not the one we'd had in the restaurant after I offered him Bernie Glassman's definition of *emptiness*. His reasoning seemed almost bizarre until I realized that the word *ineffable* was a remnant of it. Its primary meaning, according to *The American Heritage Dictionary*, is "beyond expression, indescribable." Thus, it was virtually synonymous with the definition of emptiness I'd remembered my teacher offering me and, at our dinner, I'd offered Mailer. Now, as Mailer remembered it, it referred to the condition he'd recommended to his "Buddhist friend," who'd so annoyed him with his obsession with nothingness. In effect, he'd completely distorted and inverted our discussion, forgotten the fact that his "Buddhist friend" had often noted that nothingness was *not* the focus of Buddhism and referred him to a definition of *emptiness* that was synonymous with *ineffable*. Finally, too, he had forgotten that the ineffable was not something Buddhists search for, but something they believe to be essential reality, an inescapable truth that is obscured by dualistic mind. The bottom line, however, was that, inverting our discussion in his memory, he had placed himself in a position of authority, offering—and distorting—the definition I'd offered him. It was as if the obscurations of our conversation as it traveled through his mind were finally a mirror of the circular game we'd played with our thumbs, and I had been his adversary.

Roshi shows little sign of his eighty years, but six weeks from now, after his return to Japan, he'll be found dead on the floor of his room at the monastery. He'll be five years younger than Beckett was when he died twenty-six years ago, four younger than Mailer, when he died eight years ago, two younger than I am as I write these words. He's always made a joke of his death—"Please you feed my body to the fishes!"—but the joke will be lost on us, of course, when word of his death comes from Japan. "Internal bleeding," is the coroner's explanation.

Almost as shocking as his death is the news from Kazuko—to whom, as we're soon to learn, he confided his decision just a few days before this sesshin began—that he had decided that this would be our last sesshin together. The zendo is to be closed. He has concluded that he is too old to make this trip, and there is no one among us that he believes worthy to succeed him. He is done with us—or done at least with those of us (like me) who aren't prepared to make the trip to Japan to study with him at Ryutaku-ji—and the room in which we sit is done as well. Four months from now, it will be sold on the open market, the considerable sum it fetches sent to Ryutaku-ji. The cushions on which we sit will be ours to take home or give to friends. On a Sunday afternoon in January, every item in this loft, including his private possessions—incense bowls, water bowls, favorite tea cup, L. L. Bean jacket, incense case, beloved vacuum cleaner, even the bell and sticks with which he began our sitting tonight—will be spread out on this floor as if in a flea market, and all of our members will be invited to stop by and take what they want. I'll leave with his incense case, his rice cooker, and of course the Yankee cap he was wearing when, as I described in the opening pages of *Ambivalent Zen*, we went out for breakfast twenty-four years ago.

But as far as we know, he's healthy tonight. Tomorrow evening and every evening after, he'll meet with us in private interviews, and every day he'll give a talk that will be as vibrant and funny and profound as any we've heard from him before.

As it happened, one of Beckett's production assistants on the *Endgame* rehearsals was a puppeteer who had done several productions of Beckett plays with his puppets as cast. When rehearsals ended, there was a closing party, and he was asked to give a performance of *Act Without Words*. As anyone knows who's seen it, no Beckett play demonstrates better the consistency of his vision and the relentlessness with which he maintained it. It's a silent, almost Keatonesque, litany about the futility of hope. A man sits beside a barren tree in what seems to be a desert, a blistering sun overhead. Suddenly, offstage, a whistle is heard and a glass of water descends. When he reaches for it, it rises until it's just out of reach. He stretches and strains for it, but it rises to elude him once again. Finally, he gives up and resumes his position beneath the tree. A moment later, the whistle sounds again, and a stool descends to rekindle his hope. In a flurry of excitement, he mounts the stool, stretches, grasps, and watches the water rise beyond his reach again. A succession of whistles and offerings follow, each arousing his hope and dashing it until at last he ceases to respond. The whistle continues to sound but he gives no sign of hearing it.

Like so much Beckett, it's the bleakest possible vision rendered in comedy nearly slapstick, and that evening, with Beckett himself and a number of children in the audience and an ingenious three-foot-tall puppet in the lead role, it had all of us, children included, laughing as if Keaton himself were performing it. When the performance ended, Beckett congratulated the puppeteer and his wife, who had assisted him, offering—with his usual diffidence and politeness—but a single criticism. "The whistle isn't shrill enough."

As it happened, the puppeteer's wife was a Buddhist, a follower of the path we're pursuing in sesshin, the path to which Beckett himself paid homage in his early book on Proust, when he wrote, "The wisdom of all the sages, from Brahma to Leopardi...consists not in the satisfaction but the ablation of desire."* As a devotee and a Beckett admirer, she was understandably anxious to confirm what she, like

*Samuel Beckett, *Proust* (New York: Grove Press, 1975), 18.

many others, took to be his sympathies with her religion. In fact, not a few critical opinions had been mustered, over the years, concerning his debt to Buddhism, Taoism, Zen, the Noh theater, all of it received—as it was now received from the puppeteer's wife—with curiosity, appreciation, and absolute denial by the man it presumed to explain. "I know nothing of Buddhism," he said. "If it's present in this play, it is unbeknownst to me."

Once it had been asserted, however, there remained the possibility of unconscious predilection—innate Buddhism, so to speak—so the woman had another question, which had stirred in her mind, she said, since the first time she'd seen the play. "When all is said and done, isn't this man, having given up hope, finally liberated?"

Beckett looked at her with a pained expression. He'd had his share of drink that night but not enough to make him forget his vision or push him beyond his profound resistance to hurting anyone's feelings. "Oh no," he said. "He's finished."

SIX

Among other things, a sesshin is a social experiment in an ideal laboratory. How better to explore the social matrix than by putting twenty people who agree to silence and are committed to spiritual practice in a space of twelve hundred feet for a week? Strip them of habit and routine, domestic comfort and relationship, take away their choice in what and when to eat and block their access to digital and other addictions, not to mention the work that supports, fulfills, or frustrates them. Disrupt their sleeping, snacking, and defecation habits. Wake them at five in the morning, bring them to their cushions and a blank wall ten hours a day, leave them at the mercy of their brains, minds, and feelings about each other. See how often they connect, collide, or panic. How much love they feel for each other, how much anger, fear, resentment, paranoia, lust, joy, compassion. How much they change as the week goes on and the boundaries between them thicken or disappear. How often they feel that they've arrived here at last.

Roshi rings a different, larger bell to wake us. We have thirty minutes to repack our bedrolls, get to the toilet, slap water on our face and brush our teeth, change into our sitting clothes, and, working together, rearrange the cushions we've slept on. Neatly, of course, *exactly* six feet from the wall we face and *exactly* in line with each other. Incense is already burning, its fragrance pervading and settling the room. By 5:25, be on your cushion. Do not under any circumstance be late.

At 5:30, the first of our three morning sittings begins with another sound of the bell. After the third sitting, we have a simple breakfast, which is no less formal, silent, and orderly than our sitting but—unlike at many other Zen centers and monasteries—devoid of ritual and liturgy.

Most of us eat with a bundled nest of black lacquer bowls, called *oryoki*, which Roshi brought to us from Japan. The bowls are wrapped in brown napkins, covered with a larger cloth of the same color, and include a set of chopsticks in a black pouch. We unwrap the napkin and spread our bowls on them, then take them to the kitchen, serve ourselves, and bring them back to our cushions. When Roshi rings the bell again, we eat in silence together—no less attentive to each bite than we are to each breath when we meditate. As Roshi often reminds us, eating is a continuation of our practice. Pursued with such concentration, it is vivid and intense. Though simple and unvaried, meals during sesshin can seem a first-time experience, a rediscovery of taste and texture and the pleasure you've missed in the compulsive, distracted eating habits of your ordinary life. When we're done, a pot of hot water is passed around, and, after cleaning the chopsticks and bowls with our fingertips, we dry the oryoki items with a small dish cloth we've packed with them, rewrap them carefully and neatly. Finally, an empty bowl is passed around for waste water. Unless you're a beginner, you know that the water you pour into this bowl must not contain even the tiniest scrap of food. Roshi explodes at the sight of food wasted. "Whoever leave this food losing lot of virtue!"

A work period follows breakfast. We brush each cushion carefully, vacuum and mop the floors, wash the windows, clean the bathrooms, vacuum the stairs between our loft and the building's entry three floors below, sweep the sidewalk outside the building. Roshi circulates while we work, making sure we're alert to what we're doing—vacuuming, for example, along the seams in the floor rather than perpendicular to them; mopping with attention ("sincere mopping," he calls it), and, if you finish your job before others do, offering help or finding another job to do. Resting while others work is another way to make him lose his temper. "You watching others work, you losing lot of virtue!"

At ten o'clock, we turn toward the center of the room for the morning liturgy. Like everything else in his presentation of Zen to Americans, Roshi has simplified it for us, in part because our chanting is loud, and he seeks in vain to avoid disturbing the neighbors above and below us in the building. Our service is the same every day, every sesshin, and in the midst of it, for all its simplicity, one can feel the whole of our lineage present in the room. While Roshi maintains our speed and rhythm with a small wooden drum called a *mokugyo*, we chant a series of sutras in either Pali or Sino-Japanese. The meaning of the words is sometimes clear, sometimes not, but the music and rhythm we make together is hypnotic and enveloping. In fact it helps not to know the meaning of the words you chant, so you can concentrate on breathing together with the sound you make and the sound of the drum. Though the sutras progress and elaborate on the dharma vision, everything we chant, like every instant of our meditation during the course of this week, is expressed in the first sutra we chant—the *Heart Sutra*.* Though subtle and mysterious and finally (as Mailer understood) ineffable, the text is endlessly examined and pursued by scholars and teachers of Buddhism and comparative religion. It is a description of the radical understanding at the root of Buddhism, the realization of emptiness, or *sunyata*, that Avalokitesvara Bodhisattva, one of the great Buddhist heroes, arrived at while practicing zazen (here called *prajna paramita*). We recite it every day—first in Sino-Japanese, then in English. Every line expresses the vision that brought us here, the reason we take our seat on our cushions and the freedom we're offered by doing so, the inexplicable truth of the present moment, accepting things as they are. For me, this first morning, every line reminds me of Mailer—his vision of the "ineffable" and our endless arguments about Nothingness.

Avalokiteshvara Bodhisattva, the Bodhisattva of compassion, doing deep Prajna Paramita, clearly saw that the five Skandhas are Sunyata, thus transcending misfortune and suffering. O Sariputra, form is no other than Sunyata,

*Our recitations during sesshin—*The Heart Sutra, Song of Zazen*, and others—come from the Sutra Book of the New York Zendo, translated by D.T. Suzuki, and published and made available for free by The Zen Studies Society, Inc.

Sunyata is no other than form. Form is exactly sunyata, sunyata exactly form. Feeling, thought, volition and consciousness are likewise like this. O Sariputra, remember, Dharma is fundamentally Sunyata. No birth, no death, nothing is defiled, nothing is pure. Nothing can increase, nothing can decrease. Hence: in Sunyata, no form, no feeling, no thought, no volition, no consciousness; no eyes, no ears, no tongue, no body, no mind, no seeing, no hearing, no smelling, no tasting, no touching, no thinking, no world of sight, no world of consciousness, no ignorance and no end to ignorance; no old age and death and no end to old age and death. No suffering, no craving, no extinction, no path, no wisdom, no attainment. Indeed, there is nothing to be attained. The Bodhisattva relies on Prajna Paramita with no hindrance in the mind. No hindrance, therefore no fear. Far beyond upside down views, at last Nirvana. Past, present and future, all Buddhas, Bodhissattvas rely on Prajna Paramita and therefore reach the most supreme enlightenment. Therefore know: Prajna Paramita is the greatest Dharani, the brightest Dharani, the highest Dharani, the incomparable Dharani. It completely clears all suffering. This is the truth, not a lie. So set forth the Prajna Paramita Dharani. Set forth this Dharani and say: Ga Te Ga Te Pa Ra Ga Te Para Sam Gat Te, Bhodhi Sva Ha. Heart Su Tra.

Though it feels painfully slow and plodding in the first couple of days, our schedule seems to accelerate, becoming almost comforting as the days go by. In retrospect, it can seem as if the whole week passed in the blink of an eye. We sit from 10:30 a.m. till 12:30 p.m. and then have our biggest meal: Roshi's miso soup, which is the best I've ever tasted; rice cooked according to the recipe at Ryutaku-ji (also the best I've ever had); salad prepared by Kazuko or one of the other students who's been assigned to kitchen detail. In the years since Roshi arrived in New York, the menu hasn't changed. After lunch, a ninety-minute rest period hopefully allows us to catch up on our sleep, but on this first day, for me at least, it is filled by another rush of thought and memory, no sleep at all. At 1:30, after the rest period ends, we return to our cushions for tea. Roshi makes delicious sencha, the tea he's brought from Japan, and brings it from the kitchen himself. As the pot is passed from cushion to cushion, it is followed by a bowl of cookies—Pepperidge Farm, of course. One cookie for each of us, great excitation as the bowl approaches, ridiculous impatience as one waits for Roshi to ring the bell that grants first-sip, first-bite permission. Oppressed as I am on this first day by the routine and deprivation of sesshin, the combination of sencha's caffeine and this single hit of sugar and chocolate produces a rush of energy that seems like a flash of coffee. My confidence returns. For a moment, once again, I'm happy to be here. I cannot doubt that most others in this room eat and drink with equal excitement.

After tea, we enter upon a recitation in English, one of two readings we'll alternate from day to day. Each is profound, a great Zen classic, well known not just to us but to any student of Buddhism. As usual, we begin with "Song of Zazen," by one of our most important ancestors, Hakuin Zenji. Of all our readings, it has always been the most helpful and profound for me. On this first day I hardly notice what I'm reading, but I do get flashes, single phrases or sentences, just enough to make me realize how far from Hakuin I am as I read.

> If you concentrate within and testify to the truth that Self-Nature is no Nature, you have really gone beyond foolish thought.
>
> …
>
> The thought of no thought is thought. The form of no-form is form.
>
> …
>
> At this moment, what more need we seek? This very body is the body of the Buddha.

Any one of these lines, properly understood and embraced, is a summation of what we're doing here, what Zen and Buddhism are all about. I have chanted them many times over the years, but on this first day they only remind me that I am not yet in sesshin. The self-nature that Hakuin calls "no nature" remains quite the opposite for me. I want the self I've left behind—can't bear the distance I feel from it. I'll need a lot more sitting to see that the thought of no-thought is thought. Just now, I'm exclusively fixed on the thought of no-thought. There is no indication of awareness beyond the fixation. Does it help if now and then I think about emptiness? How can I be surprised that I think of Mailer so often? I'm no less attached to my dualistic mind than he was.

After the reading, Roshi gives a talk or what—to signify that it's not a lecture but a spontaneous presentation of his practice—we call a *teisho*. Most days, it is based on one of a series of koans called the *Mumonkan* in Japanese, the *Gateless Gate* in English.* He'll use them as a launching pad and then improvise around them. Since koans are alogical, they are not answered rationally or intellectually but, as the word *teisho* reminds us, with the energy, immediacy, and

---

*Since many teachers have taught from it, many versions of the *Mumonkan* have been published. The version we've studied at Soho Zendo is: Zenkei Shibayama, *The Gateless Barrier: Zen Comments on the Mumonkan*, trans. Sumiko Kudo (Boulder CO: Shambhala, 2000).

concreteness of zazen itself. Most teachers take on these koans many times. Like his peers and predecessors, Roshi's teishos will always be spontaneous and free-associative. It is no exaggeration to say that he is answering the koan each time he speaks of it. His interpretations of any particular koan can differ as much from those of other teachers as they do from previous teishos he's given on it.

For his first teisho, he chooses "Gutei's One Finger," a famous koan that is familiar to most of us in the room.

"Today I read *Gateless Gate* case three." Since he doesn't trust his English pronunciation, he passes the book to me, sitting on his right. "Larry-san, please you read."

I take the book and read aloud:

Master Gutei, whenever he was questioned, just stuck up one finger.

At one time he had a young attendant, whom a visitor asked, "What is the Zen your Master is teaching?" The boy also stuck up one finger. Hearing of this, Gutei cut off the boy's finger with a knife. As the boy ran out screaming with pain, Gutei called to him. When the boy turned his head, Gutei stuck up his finger. The boy was suddenly enlightened.

When Gutei was about to die, he said to the assembled monks, "I attained Tenryu's Zen of One Finger. I used it all through my life, but could not exhaust it." When he had finished saying this, he died.*

On the second day, Roshi's choice is a koan that has been very important to me. He once assigned it to me and, after I worked on it in vain for almost a year, could not resist giving me the answer. That answer, and the question that precedes it, have remained as dramatic and instructive as they were when he first assigned it to me. As I listen to his teisho, I will feel, as often, that I understand it for the first time.

"Today," he says, "case five, 'Hang from a Tree.' Larry-san, please you read."

I take the book again.

Master Kyogen said, "It is like a man up a tree who hangs from a branch by his mouth; his hands cannot grasp a bough, his feet cannot touch the tree. Another man comes under the tree and asks him the meaning of Bodhidharma's coming from the West. If he does not answer, he does not meet the questioner's need. If he answers, he will lose his life. At such a time, how should he answer?"†

*Shibayama, *Gateless Barrier*, 42.
†Shibayama, *Gateless Barrier*, 53.

After teisho, we have two more sittings and then dinner, which as usual is a mix of lunch leftovers with fruit salad for dessert. Another rest period follows dinner, during which we're allowed to go out for walks in the neighborhood. Of course you try to remain in sesshin as you walk, keep your eyes from wandering. If you're not successful, you pay a price for it. Anything your eye comes to rest on can reawaken the desire you're trying to erase on your cushion. Returning to this loft after a trip in the Phenomenal World can seem like reentering a submarine which is already in deep dive. After my first, distracted walk on the first night, I vow not to go out again until sesshin is over, but the urge to go out is too strong to resist. After dinner, every evening, I slip into my street clothes and return to the world outside.

During this rest period, the dressing room has been emptied, cleaned, and set up for our interviews with Roshi—two cushions facing each other. In many Zen centers or monasteries, especially those of the Rinzai school, interviews with the master or teacher are frequent. Sometimes, they can occur twice a day. As often, Roshi's style with them is unconventional. Believing that they can distract us from the sitting, which is our main purpose here, he limits interviews to one for each of us on alternate days. There is no interview on the first day, so we meet with him three times at most over the course of the week.

In monasteries, these meetings are called *dokusan*, but Roshi calls them *kansho*. The name refers to the bell we ring twice before entering the room.* With a cushion just in front of it, it's set up in the hall outside the room. Another of the treasures he brought from Japan, it hangs from a carved wooden stand about a foot in height. You strike it with a small wooden mallet, and the way you do so—the force and arc of your hand, the gap between first and second strike, and so on—will vary according to your state of mind. Weak and frightened, distracted, anxious, egoistic and vain, calm and confident, present at the moment or somewhere else—as Roshi often reminds us, he will clearly perceive, when he hears the sound behind the closed door of the kansho room, the current state of your practice.

The interview itself can vary in length from a few seconds to ten or fifteen minutes. Longer meetings usually indicate breakthroughs in practice or psychological breakdowns that require Roshi's therapeutic support. With another bell that stands beside his cushion, he ends your interview and invites the next in line to announce him- or herself with those two all-revealing strikes of the bell. Let

---

*In Japan, the kansho is called the "calling bell." Its ringing marks the beginning of funeral services. The kansho is rung to begin the service because it is a reminder of the way that Shakyamuni Buddha shared the dharma, or teachings, with all and how it called everyone to explore the truth.

no one say that Zen, as Roshi likes to believe and often asserts, is minimal about its ritual.

My first meeting with him occurs on the second night. Though sesshin until now has been stressful and confusing, I'm actually a little high as I approach this first encounter. Early in the last sitting, I remembered a statement by Dogen—"Practice itself is enlightenment"—and realized that it applies as much to my work as zazen. It wasn't the first time I'd made the connection, but it seemed to be so. A series of insights followed. In my office, as on my cushion, it's the process that matters. What I'm doing from moment to moment, word to word, sentence to sentence— why should I think it different from the breath I follow on my cushion? My problem is I've been too goal-oriented, focusing on the book as a finished product, ignoring the great adventure I face every time I sit at my desk, not to mention the joy I find in facing it. No wonder I've been so frustrated and depressed! If I take Dogen's point of view to my desk, I'll feel as happy there as I do (sometimes, anyway) on my cushion!

I strike the bell twice, enter the room, and, following the ritual, drop to my knees, place my head on the floor, and lift my hands beside my ears. Excitement with my insight makes me impatient as I rise from the prostration and take my seat on the cushion before him. Our knees are almost touching. I look into his eyes. "I've had an amazing insight, Roshi."

He closes his eyes for a moment and then rings his bell to dismiss me and summon the next student. A moment later, I'm back on my cushion, my insight nowhere in evidence.

The fourth day, as usual, is the hardest. Now and then I let go—but not quite. Pain intensifies and moves around— back, knee, neck, and always, of course, the mind. Thought accelerates. Zen has never been so clear, so tantalizing, so stupid and self-indulgent. From moment to moment, it seems impossible, impossible to doubt, absolutely clear, hopelessly confused. As Dogen often stated, Zen is nothing but a practice in faith. Faith? It seems to me I've experienced it again and again during these first days, but of course my memories of it are nowhere near it and my yearning to find it again seems only to make it less likely. My yearning for it is very intense but self-conscious and intellectual. Is it possible that nothing contradicts faith like the idea of it? I have a mind to ask Roshi that question when I meet with him that evening in kansho, but again he rings me out as soon I take my seat in front of him.

The fifth day and the sixth seem to take their cue from his dismissal. My mind seems dull and empty, void of energy. I've not forgotten the many times I've seen this void produce insight and exhilaration, but the memory sends me deeper into the void. Thoughts about emptiness seem vivid and profound and, a moment later, hollow and pretentious. I have a chance to meet with Roshi that evening, but I cannot bring myself to do so. My years of Zen have often brought me to this nadir, but it seems more perilous this time, a slope on which I can't find grip or purchase. I try to blame my contradictions on my brain, thoughts of brain damage looming almost happily for a moment, but they are clearly strategic, disingenuous. I've often turned against Zen, but it's never frightened me so much, never seemed to me so circular and seductive, so elusive, so magnetic. Is it possible that real brain damage is the dream of freedom from the brain? What's more egoistic than ideas of compassion and altruism? What's more self-conscious? How on earth did it ever occur to me that I knew more about Zen than Mailer, not to mention Beckett?

THE LAST TIME I met Beckett was at lunch in Paris in 1984—five years after our first meeting in London—at the hotel restaurant, near his apartment, that he'd always preferred. He was as warm and friendly as always but much frailer, unsteady on his feet. As usual, he plied me with questions about my work, wanted to know if I was "still looking at the wall." Of his own work, he said, as usual, that it was going nowhere. "I've written nothing worth keeping since *Worstward Ho* last year." Not for the first time, he mentioned that a single sentence had haunted him for years: "One night, as he sat, with his head in his hands, he saw himself rise and go."

As before, he let it hang that afternoon, but the image would eventually evolve into one of the thirty-one fragments of his last published work, *Stirrings Still*. "One night, as he sat, with his head in his hands, he saw himself rise and go.... Seen always from behind whithersoever he went, he wears the same hat and coat as of old when he walked the roads. The back roads."*

Stirrings Still, a three-part prose poem, would be published a year before his death, in 1988. Shortly before that, he wrote me, in his last note, that he'd moved into a "Maison de ratraite" called Tiers Temps. It was a home for the elderly not far from the apartment he'd shared with his wife for the last twenty-five years. Barney Rosset, his devoted publisher and friend, would soon meet with him there to deliver the proofs of *Stirrings Still*.

I was never able to visit him there, but I know from the notes of those who did that his room was elemental, almost monastic—one bed, one chair, one table—accessible to a small courtyard with a single tree and pigeons he was

---

*Samuel Beckett, *Stirrings Still* (New York: Foxrock Books, 2015), 12–13.

fond of feeding. There were of course a number of other residents, aged and/or infirm. Since he was a wealthy man by this time, most of his friends found the situation unsuitable, but he was comfortable there. As his biographer Anthony Cronin noted, "With one side of his nature, he had always had a surprising need of people; and it is possible that he found the rather intimate arrangements and little rituals of...Tiers Temps, including the presence of the other inmates when he left his room, soothing and comforting. The simply furnished room and simple regimen...were somehow in tune with his rejection of the vanities of the world, and with the spirit of his work."

Though at first he considered Tier Temps a temporary expedient, he soon began to consider it his home for the foreseeable future. In fact, he would never leave it. One of his last visitors, the Irish poet Derek Mahon, spending half an hour over a glass of Jameson's with him, was impressed by his self-sufficiency: "He seemed buoyant, if unsteady on his feet, and tremendously relaxed, as if to demonstrate the logic of his previous *paean a l'outrance*, the older you get the better it felt. It seemed to me he was unquestionably having fun as the corporeal envelope disintegrated and the end drew nigh. He positively twinkled."*

Buoyant though he was, he was sinking rapidly. His

---

*Anthony Cronin, *Samuel Beckett: The Last Modernist* (New York: HarperCollins, 1996), 18.

respiratory problems were increasing. In early December he was taken to the hospital, and after several weeks of fitful consciousness, he died on December 22, 1989. In his summation of this moment, Cronin reminds us of two sentences from Beckett's book on Proust, written fifty-five years before, when he was thirty-one. "Whatever opinion we may be pleased to hold on the subject of death, we may be sure that it is meaningless and valueless. Death has not required us to keep a day free."*

THE SCHEDULE is different on our last day. A brief cleaning period follows breakfast and then a brief morning service, a teisho, and finally, two periods of zazen in which we'll each of us have a chance to meet with Roshi again. For his teisho, he chooses another famous koan. "Today I talk case twelve. 'Zuigan Osho Calls to Himself.'" He hands the book to me. "Larry-san, please you read."

> Every day Master Zuigan Shigen used to call out to himself, "Oh, Master!" and would answer himself, "Yes?" "Are you awake?" he would ask, and would answer, "Yes, I am." "Never be deceived by others, any day, any time." "No, I will not."†

---

*Cronin, *Samuel Beckett*, 592. Quoted from Beckett, *Proust*, 17.
†Shibayama, *Gateless Barrier*, 91.

Roshi shifts from side to side on his cushion, stretches his neck and shoulders, and then stares at us in silence for several moments. He often does this, but the stare seems much longer than usual. Finally, he says:

Your master awake. Already waken! Zuigan Osho called to himself every day, "Master!" and answered "Yes sir!" Maybe you think, "Who is calling, who answering?" Only called and "yes!" Answer "yes!" Every second individual, independent. No connection between "master!" and "yes sir!" No connection! You independent yourself! Don't think this about Zen master or karate master. Or tea master. Those are phenomenal point master. Essential point, everyone is master. If you following outside environment, you become slave. Of your ego. Your selfish. Your dualistic mentality.

His talk is shorter today—a bit less than half an hour. As usual, I understand him now and then, see exactly what he's talking about. It's essential nature to which he refers, all beings' essential nature, the essence that is formless, empty, a function of the present moment. For a moment, I get it exactly, realize as never before, with a rush of energy and happiness, my own essential nature, but then the energy void I entered yesterday engulfs me once again. Finally, it's clear to me that I've made no progress. It's all conceptual for me. Like he said, I'm a slave of my dualistic mentality. But how does it help to know it? Where is such knowledge produced if not within the brain that produces the dualism? It's a circular prison in which I'm trapped, a brain that makes everything dualistic while producing these wondrous images of nondualism, and seven days of sitting have only made it more efficient, more dogged and malicious. By the end of his talk, I feel like I'm in a wind tunnel.

After the teisho, as usual, we have a recitation, the simplest we do. It's called *The First Step in Zazen*. I've always found it simplistic, a collection of spiritual clichés, ideas that I, like everyone in this room, have entertained for years. I've never understood why Roshi includes it. Its author, however, is not one to underestimate. He is Zen master Soyen Shaku, a seminal figure in Rinzai Zen. In 1893, he was one of four priests and two laymen who represented Zen at the World Parliament of Religions in Chicago. He was D. T. Suzuki's teacher and—even more important, in the view of those, like us, who are committed to the particular path of Rinzai Zen—the pivotal master of Nyogen Senzaki. Senzaki established one of the first zendos in the United States, in San Francisco in 1922. By mail and then directly, he formed a close friendship with Soen Nakagawa Roshi, and the connection between them was crucial in the history of the Zen Studies Society and American Zen in general.*

As usual for this recitation, Roshi opens the sutra book and begins the reading. We join him in the second sentence:

Zazen is not a difficult task. Just free yourself of all incoming thoughts and hold your mind against them like a great iron wall. Think of your own room as the whole world, and that all sentient beings are sitting there with you, as one.

Make a searching analysis of yourself. Realize that your body is not your body. It is part of the whole body of sentient beings. Your mind is not your mind. It is but a constituent of all mind. Your eyes, your ears, your nose, your tongue, your hands, and your feet are not merely your individual belongings, but one in joint ownership with all sentient beings. You simply call them yours—and others. You cling to your own being and consider others separate from you. This is nothing but a baseless delusion of yours.

Just free yourself of all incoming complications and hold your mind against them like a great iron wall. No matter what sort of contending thoughts arise in you, ignore

*Senzaki was the author of *The Iron Flute,* a famous book on koans. His friendship with Soen Roshi—which originated in correspondence that began after Senzaki settled in the United States—was a significant reason for Soen's decision to teach in the United States.

them and they will perish and disappear of themselves. And just as soon as your thought expands and unites with the universe, you are free from your stubborn ego.

Then you will enter a condition where there is no relativity, no absoluteness. You are now transcendent, far above both discrimination and equality. You have nothing to receive and there is nothing to receive you. There is no time, no space. There is no past, no future, but one eternal present.

This is not the true realization, but you are walking near the palace. Just free yourself from all incoming disturbances, and hold your mind against them like a great iron wall. Then someday you will meet your true Self as if you have awakened from a dream and you will have the happiness you never could have derived otherwise.

Zazen is not a difficult task. It is a way to lead you to your long-lost home.

Knowing the lines by heart, I recite them with fleeting attention, expecting nothing. After all, I've been reciting them for more than twenty years without particular benefit or insight. Why expect more this morning?

But the dullness of the recitation has somehow relieved the dullness of my mind. When I turn to face the wall again, one line persists: "Zazen is a way to lead you to your long-lost home." How is it I've never made this connection?

Zazen is home and home is zazen and where else, after all, do I want to be? This breath is home. *Now* is home. This breath and this breath and this breath. Obvious though it is, the connection has energy and velocity that circulates in my body. It seems to me I've never known *home* before. What is it but the present moment, things as they are, the contentment, the freedom from desire, which has suddenly enveloped me? *Now* is the only home I can know. I can't lose it and it can't be taken away. The space and time I've sought for years is the one I'm in right now. Even my brain, busy as usual, is home. The thoughts it's generating are happening now. THIS is the only home I'll ever have, the only one I want.

My stillness persists for two minutes, I'd guess, maybe a bit longer. Then all at once I begin to shake. My body seems to be invaded by an external force, an energy I can't control. The first signs of it are slight tremors in my feet and hands, but they quickly proliferate, moving into my forearms, my calves, my neck. Soon I'm enveloped by tremors that seem almost epileptic. My body seems like a battleground, separate from me and out of control.

The shaking continues for several moments but then stops as suddenly as it began. The cessation is almost as disorienting as the attack it replaced, but after a moment, I feel at home again, suffused again with tranquility and happiness. How is it possible that such a storm has left no damage in its wake? If anything, the stillness I feel is deeper than before.

It takes but a moment to understand what happened. It's obvious, isn't it? The contentment I felt—and feel again—is nothing less than the essential nature that Roshi is always directing us to acknowledge. But essential nature, as he reminds us, is formless, and the brain of course deals only in form. Again I see what I've seen so often—nothing disturbs the brain like emptiness, and emptiness is nothing but the present moment, things as they are. Isn't this the brain damage I've suspected all along? The frantic insistence on form that zazen challenges? Isn't this why I've had so much trouble with my book? Books are form. *This* is empty. Mailer and Beckett were all about form. Beckett fought it, Mailer embraced it, but different as they were, they were locked in the same dilemma, obedient to their brains. And I'm no different! How can I pretend that I've approached the truth that Roshi teaches? The "long-lost home" I knew a moment ago—what was it but freedom from brain damage, the endless desire my brain is programmed to produce? The shaking was its response to contentment, the formless condition it can't tolerate. For the first time in my life, I knew total freedom from brain damage, but my brain rejected the cure it was offered!

Two hours later, before the lunch that will terminate sesshin, I have my last interview with Roshi—the last, in fact, that I'll ever have with him. In all the years I've studied with him, I've never been so impatient to see him. The words explode the moment I sit down. Home and shaking, home and emptiness, not-home, shaking again and home again—I describe the whole of my journey to him. "At last I got it, Roshi. Everything you've been teaching us. Essential nature. My long-lost home. I got there at last. But home is empty, and the brain makes form. Of course, it could not accept what I found. That's why I started to shake. Home humiliated my brain! I got there at last, Roshi! That's why I was shaking!"

Roshi shuts his eyes for a moment and then fixes them on me.

"Larry-san?"

"Yes?"

"Shaking is your long-lost home."

ACKNOWLEDGMENTS

A BOOK LIKE THIS could not be written without assistance and generosity encountered along the way. For critical reading when I needed it most, I want to express my appreciation to my wife, Vivian Bower, my friends, Andra Samelson, Rudy Wurlitzer, Tatjana Krizmanic, Helen Tworkov, Steve Shainberg, and Michael Lennon, and my editors, Matt Zepelin and Audra Figgins.

Finally, I offer endless gratitude to my teacher, Kyudo Nakagawa Roshi, Norman Mailer, and Samuel Beckett, who for all their differences shared a wisdom and generosity which illuminated countless lives they touched. In a life of endless good fortune, knowing them remains a stroke of luck from which I've never ceased to benefit.